CBSE Term II
2022

Psychology
Class XII

CBSE Term II 2022

Psychology
Class XII

- Complete Theory Covering NCERT
- Cased Based Questions
- Short/Long Answer Type Questions
- 3 Practice Papers with Explanations

Authors

Tushar Shukla *(M.A. Psychology)*

Dr. Abha Bedi Dhamija
(B.D.S (Gold Medalist), M.A. Psychology)

ARIHANT PRAKASHAN (School Division Series)

arihant

ARIHANT PRAKASHAN (School Division Series)

卐 **Administrative & Production Offices**

Regd. Office

'Ramchhaya' 4577/15, Agarwal Road, Darya Ganj, New Delhi -110002
Tele: 011- 47630600, 43518550

卐 **Head Office**

Kalindi, TP Nagar, Meerut (UP) - 250002, Tel: 0121-7156203, 7156204

卐 **Sales & Support Offices**

Agra, Ahmedabad, Bengaluru, Bareilly, Chennai, Delhi, Guwahati, Hyderabad, Jaipur, Jhansi, Kolkata, Lucknow, Nagpur & Pune.

卐 **ISBN :** 978-93-25797-04-8

PO No : TXT-XX-XXXXXXX-X-XX

Published by Arihant Publications (India) Ltd.

For further information about the books published by Arihant, log on to www.arihantbooks.com or e-mail at info@arihantbooks.com

Follow us on   

Contents

Syllabus

CBSE Term II ClassXII

Unit/Topic	Periods	Marks
1. Psychological Disorders	24	13

The topics in this unit are:

1. Introduction

2. Concepts of Abnormality and Psychological Disorders
   - Historical Background

3. Classification of Psychological Disorders

4. Factors Underlying Abnormal Behaviour

5. Major Psychological Disorders
   - Anxiety Disorders
   - Obsessive-Compulsive and Related Disorders
   - Trauma-and Stressor-Related Disorders
   - Somatic Symptom and Related Disorders
   - Dissociative Disorders
   - Depressive Disorder
   - Bipolar and Related Disorders
   - Schizophrenia Spectrum and Other Psychotic Disorders
   - Neurodevelopmental Disorders
   - Disruptive, Impulse-Control and Conduct Disorders
   - Feeding and Eating Disorders
   - Substance Related and Addictive Disorders

Unit/Topic	Periods	Marks

2. Therapeutic Approaches
The topics in this unit are:
 	
1. Nature and Process of Psychotherapy
  • Therapeutic relationship
 	
2. Types of Therapies
  • Behaviour Therapy
  • Cognitive Therapy
  • Humanistic-Existential Therapy
  • Alternative Therapies
 	
3. Rehabilitation of the Mentally Ill
	16	7

3. Attitude and Social Cognition
The topics in this unit are:
 	
1. Introduction
2. Explaining Social Behaviour
3. Nature and Components of Attitudes
4. Attitude Formation and Change
  • Attitude Formation
  • Attitude Change
  • Attitude-Behaviour Relationship
5. Prejudice and Discrimination
6. Strategies for Handling Prejudice
	12	8

4. Social Influence and Group Processes
The topics in this unit are:
 	
1. Introduction
2. Nature and Formation of Groups
3. Type of Groups
4. Influence of Group on Individual Behaviour
  • Social Loafing
  • Group Polarization
	8	7

CBSE Circular

Acad - 51/2021, 05 July 2021

Exam Scheme Term I & II

केन्द्रीय माध्यमिक शिक्षा बोर्ड
(शिक्षा मंत्रालय, भारत सरकार के अधीन एक स्वायत संगठन)

CENTRAL BOARD OF SECONDARY EDUCATION
(An Autonomous Organisation under the Ministryof Education, Govt. of India)

CBSE/DIR (ACAD)/2021

Date: July 05, 2021
Circular No: Acad-51/2021

All the Heads of Schools affiliated to CBSE

Subject: Special Scheme of Assessment for Board Examination Classes X and XII for the Session 2021-22

COVID 19 pandemic caused almost all CBSE schools to function in a virtual mode for most part of the academic session of 2020-21. Due to the extreme risk associated with the conduct of Board examinations during the second wave in April 2021, CBSE had to cancel both its class X and XII Board examinations of the year 2021 and results are to be declared on the basis of a credible, reliable, flexible and valid alternative assessment policy. This, in turn, also necessitated deliberations over alternative ways to look at the learning objectives as well as the conduct of the Board Examinations for the academic session 2021-22 in case the situation remains unfeasible.

CBSE has also held stake holder consultations with Government schools as well as private independent schools from across the country especially schools from the remote rural areas and a majority of them have requested for the rationalization of the syllabus, similar to last year in view of reduced time permitted for organizing online classes. The Board has also considered the concerns regarding differential availability of electronic gadgets, connectivity and effectiveness of online teaching and other socio-economic issues specially with respect to students from economically weaker section and those residing in far flung areas of the country. In a survey conducted by CBSE, it was revealed that the rationalized syllabus notified for the session 2020-21 was effective for schools in covering the syllabus and helped learners in achieving learning objectives in a less stressful manner.

In the above backdrop and in line with the Board's continued focus on assessing stipulated learning outcomes by making the examinations competencies and core concepts based, student-centric, transparent, technology-driven, and having advance provision of alternatives for different future scenarios, the following schemes are introduced for the Academic Session for Class X and Class XII 2021-22.

Special Scheme for 2021-22

A. Academic session to be divided into 2 Terms with approximately 50% syllabus in each term:

The syllabus for the Academic session 2021-22 will be divided into 2 terms by following a systematic approach by looking into the interconnectivity of concepts and topics by the Subject Experts and the Board will conduct examinations at the end of each term on the basis of the bifurcated syllabus. This is done to increase the probability of having a Board conducted classes X and XII examinations at the end of the academic session.

B. The syllabus for the Board examination 2021-22 will be rationalized similar to that of the last academic session to be notified in July 2021. For academic transactions, however, schools will follow the curriculum and syllabus released by the Board vide Circular no. F.1001/CBSE-Acad/Curriculum/2021 dated 31 March 2021. Schools will also use alternative academic calendar and inputs from the NCERT on transacting the curriculum.

C. Efforts will be made to make Internal Assessment/ Practical/ Project work more credible and valid as per the guidelines and Moderation Policy to be announced by the Board to ensure fair distribution of marks.

Details of Curriculum Transaction

- Schools will continue teaching in distance mode till the authorities permit in-person mode of teaching in schools.

- **Classes IX-X: Internal Assessment** (throughout the year-irrespective of Term I and II) would include the *3 periodic tests, student enrichment, portfolio and practical work/ speaking listening activities/ project.*

- **Classes XI-XII: Internal Assessment** (throughout the year-irrespective of Term I and II) would include end of topic or unit tests/ exploratory activities/ practicals/ projects.

- Schools would create a student profile for all assessment undertaken over the year and retain the evidences in digital format.

- CBSE will facilitate schools to upload marks of Internal Assessment on the CBSE IT platform.

- Guidelines for Internal Assessment for all subjects will also be released along with the rationalized term wise divided syllabus for the session 2021-22.The Board would also provide additional resources like sample assessments, question banks, teacher training etc. for more reliable and valid internal assessments.

केन्द्रीय माध्यमिक शिक्षा बोर्ड
(शिक्षा मंत्रालय, भारत सरकार के अधीन एक स्वायत संगठन)
CENTRAL BOARD OF SECONDARY EDUCATION
(An Autonomous Organisation under the Ministryof Education, Govt. of India)

<u>Term I Examinations:</u>

- At the end of the first term, the Board will organize **Term I Examination** in a flexible schedule to be conducted between November-December 2021 with a window period of 4-8 weeks for schools situated in different parts of country and abroad. Dates for conduct of examinations will be notified subsequently.

- The Question Paper will have Multiple Choice Questions (MCQ) including case-based MCQs and MCQs on assertion-reasoning type. Duration of test will be **90 minutes** and it will cover only the rationalized syllabus of **Term I only** (i.e. approx. 50% of the entire syllabus).

- Question Papers will be sent by the CBSE to schools along with marking scheme.

- The exams will be conducted under the supervision of the External Center Superintendents and Observers appointed by CBSE.

- The responses of students will be captured on OMR sheets which, after scanning may be directly uploaded at CBSE portal or alternatively may be evaluated and marks obtained will be uploaded by the school on the very same day. The final direction in this regard will be conveyed to schools by the Examination Unit of the Board.

- Marks of the **Term I** Examination will contribute to the final overall score of students.

<u>Term II Examination/ Year-end Examination:</u>

- At the end of the second term, the Board would organize **Term II or Year-end Examination** based on the rationalized syllabus of Term II only (i.e. approximately 50% of the entire syllabus).

- This examination would be held around **March-April 2022** at the examination centres fixed by the Board.

- The paper will be of **2 hours duration** and have questions of different formats (case-based/ situation based, open ended- short answer/ long answer type).

- In case the situation is not conducive for normal descriptive examination **a 90 minute MCQ based exam** will be conducted at the end of the Term II also.

- Marks of the Term II Examination would contribute to the final overall score.

केन्द्रीय माध्यमिक शिक्षा बोर्ड

(शिक्षा मंत्रालय, भारत सरकार के अधीन एक स्वायत संगठन)

CENTRAL BOARD OF SECONDARY EDUCATION

(An Autonomous Organisation under the Ministryof Education, Govt. of India)

<u>Assessment / Examination as per different situations</u>

A. In case the situation of the pandemic improves and students are able to come to schools or centres for taking the exams.

Board would conduct Term I and Term II examinations at schools/centres and the theory marks will be distributed equally between the two exams.

B. In case the situation of the pandemic forces complete closure of schools during November-December 2021, but Term II exams are held at schools or centres.

Term I MCQ based examination would be done by students online/offline from home - in this case, the weightage of this exam for the final score would be reduced, and weightage of Term II exams will be increased for declaration of final result.

C. In case the situation of the pandemic forces complete closure of schools during March-April 2022, but Term I exams are held at schools or centres.

Results would be based on the performance of students on Term I MCQ based examination and internal assessments. The weightage of marks of Term I examination conducted by the Board will be increased to provide year end results of candidates.

D. In case the situation of the pandemic forces complete closure of schools and Board conducted Term I and II exams are taken by the candidates from home in the session 2021-22.

Results would be computed on the basis of the Internal Assessment/Practical/Project Work and Theory marks of Term-I and II exams taken by the candidate from home in Class X / XII subject to the moderation or other measures to ensure validity and reliability of the assessment.

In all the above cases, data analysis of marks of students will be undertaken to ensure the integrity of internal assessments and home based exams.

Dr. Joseph Emmanuel
Director (Academics)

CHAPTER 01

Psychological Disorders

In this Chapter...

- Introduction
- Concept of Abnormality and Psychological Disorders
- Approaches of Abnormality
- Classification of Psychological Disorders
- Factors Underlying Abnormal Behaviour
- Major Psychological Disorders

Introduction

Psychological disorders are those mental disorders which result in certain behavioural pattern such as unhappiness, discomfort, anxiety, etc. They also lead to failure in adaptation to life challenges.

When the behaviour cannot be changed according to the needs of the situation, it becomes **maladaptive**[1]. Abnormal psychology discusses about maladaptive behaviour, its causes, consequences and treatment.

Concept of Abnormality and Psychological Disorders

The word 'abnormal' literally means 'away from the normal'. It implies deviation from some clearly defined norms or standards.

Many definitions of abnormality have been used over the years, but none is accepted universally. However, these definitions have common features known as the four D's. These four Ds' are as follows

(i) **Deviant/deviance** It means abnormality different for different people. For example, for some people it is extreme, for some it is unusual and for some it is even bizarre.

(ii) **Distressing/distress** It means abnormality is unpleasant and upsetting to the person and to others.

(iii) **Dysfunctional/dysfunction** It means interfering with the person's ability to carry out daily activities in a constructive way.

(iv) **Dangerous/danger** It can be dangerous to the person or to others.

In psychology, we have no 'ideal model' or 'normal model' of human behaviour to use as a base for comparison between normal and abnormal behaviour.

Various approaches have been used to distinguish between normal and abnormal behaviours. From these approaches, two basic and conflicting views emerged which are as follows

(i) The first approach refers to abnormal behaviour as a deviation from the social norms. Each society has norms, which are stated or unstated rules for proper conduct. Behaviours, thoughts and emotions that break societal norms are called **abnormal**.

A society's norms grow from its particular culture. Culture includes history, values, institutions, habits, skills, technology and arts.

---

1 Maladaptive Maladaptive are those behaviours which stop a person from adopting to new or difficult circumstances.

A society's values may change over time. It is based on the assumption that socially accepted behaviour is not abnormal, and that normality is nothing more than conformity to social norms.

(*ii*) The second approach views abnormal behaviour as maladaptive. Many psychologists think that the normality of behaviour does not depend on the fact whether society accepts it or not, but it depends on the well-being of the individual and group. Well-being is not only maintenance or survival, but it includes growth and fulfillment.

Historical Background of Abnormality

Ancient theory about abnormality holds that abnormal behaviour can be explained by the operation of supernatural and magical forces such as evil spirits (*bhoot-pret*) or the devil (*shaitan*). **Exorcism** i.e. removing the evil that resides in the individual through countermagic and prayer is still commonly used.

In many societies, the *shaman* or medicine man (*ojha*) is a person who is believed to have contact with supernatural forces and is the medium through which spirits communicate with human beings. It is believed that through *shaman*, an affected person can know which spirit is responsible for his/her problem and what needs to be done to make the spirit happy.

Approaches of Abnormality

Biological or Organic Approach

The history of abnormal psychology believed that individuals behave strangely because their bodies and their brains are not working properly. This is known as the biological or organic approach. In the modern era, there is an evidence that body and brain processes have been linked to many types of maladaptive behaviour. If these defective biological processes are corrected then it will result in improved functioning.

Psychological Approach

According to this point of view, psychological problems are caused by inadequacies in the way an individual thinks, feels or perceives the world. All three of these perspectives i.e. supernatural, biological or organic and psychological have recurred throughout the history of Western civilisation.

Organismic Approach

In the ancient Western world, philosopher and physicians of ancient Greece such as **Hippocrates, Socrates** and **Plato** developed the organismic approach and viewed disturbed

behaviour as arising out of conflicts between emotion and reason.

Galen elaborated the role of the **four humours** (earth, air, fire and water) in personal character and temperament. According to him, the material world was made up of earth, air, fire and water which combined to form four essential body fluids, *viz* blood, black bile, yellow bile, and phlegm. Each of these fluids was seen to be responsible for a different temperament. Imbalances among the humours were believed to cause various disorders.

This is similar to the Indian notion of the three *doshas* i.e. *vata*, *pitta* and *kapha* which were mentioned in the *Atharva Veda* and *Ayurvedic* texts.

Demonology and Superstition

* In the Middle ages, demonology was related to a belief that people with mental problems were evil. In this period, demonology and superstition gained renewed importance in the explanation of abnormal behaviour.

* During the early Middle Ages, the Christian spirit of charity was appreciated. St. Augustine wrote elaborately about feelings, mental anguish and conflict. Modern psycho-dynamic theories of abnormal behaviour has developed from it.

* The **Renaissance Period** was marked by increased humanism and curiosity about behaviour. **Johann Weyer** emphasised psychological conflict and disturbed interpersonal relationships as causes of psychological disorders. He believed that 'witches' were mentally disturbed who required medical treatment.

* The seventeenth and eighteenth centuries were known as the **Age of Reason** and **Enlightenment**, as the scientific method replaced faith and dogma (belief) as ways of understanding abnormal behaviour.

* In the eighteenth century, the growth of a scientific attitude towards psychological disorders contributed to the **Reform Movement** and increased compassion for people who suffered from these disorders.

* Reforms of asylums were initiated in both Europe and America. The aspect of the reform movement was the new inclination for **deinstitutionalisation**[2]. It placed emphasis on providing community care for recovered mentally ill individuals.

Bio-psycho-social Approach

In this approach, all three factors i.e. biological, psychological and social play important roles in influencing the expression and outcome of psychological disorders.

---

2 Deinstitutionalisation It is the transfer of former mental patients from institutions into the community.

Classification of Psychological Disorders

The **American Psychiatric Association** (APA) published an official manual describing and classifying various kinds of psychological disorders. The current version of it, the **Diagnostic and Statistical Manual of Mental Disorders, 5th Edition** (DSM-5), evaluates the patient on five dimensions rather than just one broad aspect of 'mental disorder'. These dimensions relate to biological, psychological, social and other aspects.

The classification scheme officially used in India is the tenth revision of the International Classification of Diseases, which is known as the **ICD-10 Classification of Behavioural and Mental Disorders**. It was prepared by the World Health Organisation (WHO). For each disorder, a description of the main clinical features or symptoms and other associated features including diagnostic guidelines is provided in this scheme.

Factors Underlying Abnormal Behaviour

Psychologists use different approaches to understand abnormal behaviour. These approaches also emphasise the role of different factors which are as follows

Biological Factors

These factors influence all aspects of our behaviour. A wide range of biological factors such as faulty genes, endocrine imbalances, malnutrition, injuries and other conditions may interfere with normal development and functioning of the human body. These factors may be the potential causes of abnormal behaviour.

According to the biological model, abnormal behaviour might be caused by biochemical or physiological changes. Biological researchers have found that psychological disorders are related to problems in the transmission of messages from one neuron to another.

When an electrical impulse reaches a neuron's ending, the nerve ending is stimulated to release a chemical, called a **neuro-transmitter**.

Studies indicate that abnormal activity by certain neuro-transmitters can lead to specific psychological disorders. Anxiety disorders have been linked to low activity of the neuro-transmitter **Gamma Amino Butyric Acid**[3] (GABA). Similarly, schizophrenia have been linked to excess activity of dopamine and depression have been linked to low activity of serotonin.

Genetic Factors

These factors have been linked to mood disorders, schizophrenia, mental retardation and other psychological disorders. Researchers have not been able to identify the specific genes that are the culprits. In most cases, no single gene is responsible for a particular behaviour or a psychological disorder. Infact, many genes combine to bring about our various behaviours and emotional reactions, both functional and dysfunctional.

Psychological Models

There are several psychological models which provide a psychological explanation of mental disorders. The psychological and interpersonal factors have a significant role to play in abnormal behaviour. These factors include

- Maternal deprivation (separation from the mother or lack of warmth and stimulation during early years of life).
- Faulty parent-child relationships (rejection, overpro-tection, over permissiveness, faulty discipline, etc.)
- Maladaptive family structures (inadequate or disturbed family) and severe stress.

The psychological models include the psychodynamic model, behavioural model, cognitive model, humanistic-existential model, Socio-cultural Model and Diathesis-strees Model. These are discussed as follows

Psychodynamic Model

Psychodynamic model is the oldest and most famous of the modern psychological models. Psychodynamic theorists believe that behaviour, whether normal or abnormal is determined by psychological forces within the person of which she/he is not consciously aware. These internal forces are considered dynamic i.e. they interact with one another and their interaction gives shape to behaviour, thoughts and emotions.

Abnormal symptoms are viewed as the result of conflicts between these forces. This model was first formulated by **Freud** who believed that three central forces shape the personality. These are as follows

(*i*) Instinctual needs, drives and impulses (id).

(*ii*) Rational thinking (ego).

(*iii*) Moral standards (superego).

Freud stated that abnormal behaviour is a symbolic expression of unconscious mental conflicts that can be generally traced to early childhood or infancy.

---

3 **Gamma Amino Butyric Acid** It is naturally occurring amino acid that works as a neurotransmitter in a person brain.

Behavioural Model

Behavioural model states that both normal and abnormal behaviours are learned and psychological disorders are the result of learning maladaptive ways of behaving. The model concentrates on behaviours that are learned through conditioning. It proposes that what has been learned can be unlearned. Learning can take place by the following

Classical Conditioning It is a type of learning by temporary association in which two events repeatedly occur in same time.

Operant Conditioning It is a method of learning which employs rewards and punishment for learning.

Social Learning Learning through the observation of other people's behaviour.

These three types of conditioning account for behaviour, whether adaptive or maladaptive.

Cognitive Model

Psychological factors are emphasised by the cognitive model. This model states that abnormal functioning can result from cognitive problems. People may hold assumptions and attitudes about themselves that are irrational and inaccurate. They may also repeatedly think in illogical ways. Sometimes they make overgeneralisations and draw broad, negative conclusions on the basis of a single insignificant event.

Humanistic-Existential Model

Humanistic-existential model focuses on broader aspects of human existence. Humanists believe that human beings are born with a natural tendency to be friendly, cooperative and constructive. They are driven to self-actualise i.e. to fulfil this potential for goodness and growth. Existentialists believe that from birth we have total freedom to give meaning to our existence or to avoid that responsibility. Those who avoid the responsibility would live empty, inauthentic and dysfunctional lives.

Socio-Cultural Model

Some important socio-cultural factors are war and violence, group prejudice and discrimination, economic and employment problems and rapid social change. All these can lead to psychological problems in some individuals.

According to the socio-cultural model, abnormal behaviour is best understood by the social and cultural forces that influence an individual. Factors such as family structure and communication, social networks, societal conditions and societal labels and roles become more important as these societal forces shaped the behaviour. Some family structure can produce abnormal functioning among its members. In some families, members are over involved in each other's activities, thoughts and feelings. Children from these families may face difficulty in becoming independent in life.

The broader social networks in which people operate include their social and professional relationships. People who are isolated and lack social support, i.e. strong and fulfilling interpersonal relationships in their lives are likely to become more depressed and remain depressed longer than those who have good friendships.

Diathesis-Stress Model

This model states that psychological disorders develop when a diathesis (a tendency to suffer from a particular medical condition) is set off by a stressful situation. This model has three components which are as follows

(i) The first component is the diathesis or the presence of some biological disorder which may be inherited.

(ii) The second component is that the diathesis may carry a vulnerability to develop a psychological disorder. This means that the person is 'at risk' or 'predisposed' to develop the disorder.

(iii) The third component is the presence of pathogenic stressors i.e. factors/stressors that may lead to psychopathology.

This model has been applied to several disorders including anxiety, depression, and schizophrenia.

Major Psychological Disorders

The major psychological disorders are anxiety disorders, somatoform disorders, dissociative disorders, mood disorders, schizophrenia disorders, behavioural and development disorders and substance-use disorders. These are discussed below

Anxiety Disorders

The term anxiety is usually defined as a diffuse, vague (unclear), very unpleasant feeling of fear and apprehension. The anxious individual shows combinations of the following symptoms

- Rapid heart rate
- Shortness of breath
- Diarrhoea
- Loss of appetite
- Fainting
- Dizziness
- Sweating
- Sleeplessness
- Frequent urination
- Tremors

Anxiety disorders includes the following disorders

Generalised Anxiety Disorder

It consists of continued, vague (unclear), unexplained and intense fears that are not attached to any particular object. The symptoms include nervousness and feeling of apprehension about the future; hypervigilance, which involves constantly scanning the environment for dangers. It is marked by motor tension, as a result of which the person is unable to relax, is restless and visibly shaky (weak) and tense.

Panic Disorder

It consists of recurrent anxiety attacks in which the person experiences intense terror. A panic attack denotes an abrupt rise of intense anxiety rising to a peak when thoughts of a particular stimuli are present.

Such thoughts occur in an unpredictable manner. The clinical features include shortness of breath, dizziness, trembling, palpitations , choking, nausea, chest pain or discomfort, fear of going crazy, losing control or dying.

Phobia

Individuals who have phobias have irrational fears related to specific objects, people or situations. Phobias can be grouped into three main types, i.e. specific phobias, social phobias, and agoraphobia which are discussed as follows

(i) **Specific Phobia** It is the most commonly occurring type of phobia. This group includes irrational fears such as intense fear of a certain type of animal, or of being in an enclosed space.

(ii) **Social Phobia** Intense fear and embarrassment when dealing with others characterises social phobias.

(iii) **Agoraphobia** It is the term used when people develop a fear of entering unfamiliar situations. Many agoraphobics are afraid of leaving their home. So their ability to carry out normal life activities is severely limited.

Separation Anxiety Disorder (SAD)

- Individuals with this type of disorder are fearful and anxious about separation from attachment figures to such an extent which is developmentally not appropriate. For example, children with SAD may have difficulty being in a room by themselves or going to school alone. They are fearful of entering in a new situation. They even throw severe (sudden anger by a child) and make suicidal gestures.

- The ways in which children express and experience depression are related to their level of physical, emotional and cognitive development. An infant may show sadness by being passive and unresponsive; a pre- schooler may appear withdrawn and inhibited; a school- age child may be argumentative and combative and a teenager may express feelings of guilt and hopelessness.

Obsessive-Compulsive Disorder

- People affected by obsessive-compulsive disorder are unable to control their preoccupation with specific ideas or are unable to prevent themselves from repeatedly carrying out a particular act that affect their ability to carry out normal activities.

- **Obsessive behaviour** is the inability to stop thinking about a particular idea or topic.

- **Compulsive behaviour** is the need to perform certain behaviours over and over again. Many compulsions deal with counting, ordering, checking, touching and washing. Other disorder in this category include hoarding disorder, trichotillomania (hair-pulling disorder), excoriation (skin-picking) disorder, etc.

Trauma and Stressor Related Disorders

People who have been caught in a natural disaster (such as tsunami) or have been victims of bomb blasts by terrorists or been in a serious accident or in a war-related situation, experience Post-Traumatic Stress Disorder (PTSD). PTSD symptoms may include recurrent dreams, flashbacks, impaired concentration, and emotional numbing. Adjustment Disorders and Acute Stress Disorder are also included in this category.

Major Anxiety Disorders and their Symptoms

(i) **Generalised Anxiety Disorder** : prolonged, vague, unexplained and intense fears that have no logical reason accompained by hypervigilange and moter tension.

(ii) **Panic Disorder** : frequent anxiety attacks characterised by feeling of intense terror and dread; unpredictable 'panic attacks' along with physiological symptoms like breathlessness, palpitations, trembling, dizziness and a sense of loosing control or even dying.

(iii) **Specific Phobia** : irrational fears related to specific objects, interactions with others and unfamiliar situations.

(iv) **Separation Anxiety Disorder** : extreme distress when expecting or going through separation from home or other significant people to whom the individual is immensely attached to.

(v) **Other Disorders** : included under this category are selective mutism, substance/medication induced anxiety disorder, anxiety disorder due to another medical condition, etc.

Somatic Symptom and Related Disorders

In somatoform disorders, the individual has psychological difficulties and complains of physical symptoms for which there is no biological cause.

These include somatic symptom disorder, illness anxiety and conversion disorder which are discussed as follows

Somatic Symptom Disorder

It involves a person having body-related symptoms which may or may not be related to any serious medical condition. People having this disorder always worry about their health and make frequent visit to doctors. They experience distress and disturbances in their daily life.

Illness Anxiety Disorder

It develops when the individual persistently is preoccupied with developing a serious illness and worry about it. He is always anxious about his own health.

He becomes tensed by hearing someone else's ill health or some such news. He does not respond to doctor's assurance, always thinks about undiagnosed disease and negative diagnostic results.

Both **somatic symptom disorder** and **illness anxiety disorder** are concerned with medical illness. In somatic symptom disorder, there are still physical complaints but illness anxiety disorder is purely mental.

Conversion Disorders

The symptoms of conversion disorders are the reported loss of part or all of basic body functions. Paralysis, blindness, deafness and difficulty in walking are generally among the symptoms reported. These symptoms occur after stressful experience and develop suddenly.

Dissociative Disorders

Dissociation involves feelings of unreality, estrangement (detachment), depersonalisation and sometimes a loss or shift of identity. Sudden temporary alterations of consciousness that mark out painful experiences are a defining characteristic of dissociative disorders.

Four conditions which are included in this disorder are as follows

Dissociative Amnesia

It is characterised by extensive but selective memory loss that has no known organic cause (e.g. head injury). Some people cannot remember anything about their past. Others can no longer recall specific events, people, places or objects, while their memory for other events remains intact. This disorder is often associated with an overwhelming stress.

Dissociative Fugue

It is a part of dissociative amnesia. It is characterised by the assumption of a new identity and the inability to recall the previous identity. The fugue usually ends when the person suddenly 'wakes up' with no memory of the events that occurred during the fugue. It is associated with an overwhelming stress.

Dissociative Identity Disorder

It is often referred to as multiple personality disorder and is the most dramatic of the dissociative disorders. It is often associated with traumatic experiences in childhood. In this disorder, the person assumes alternate personalities that may or may not be aware of each other.

Depersonalisation

It involves an imaginary state in which the person has a sense of being separated both from self and from reality. In depersonalisation, there is a change of self-perception and the person's sense of reality is temporarily lost or changed.

Depressive Disorders

These are characterised by disturbances in mood or continued emotional state. The most common mood disorder is **depression**. Depression covers a variety of negative moods and behavioural changes. We often use the term depression to refer to normal feelings after a significant loss, such as the break-up of a relationship or the failure to attain a significant goal.

- **Major Depressive Disorder** It is defined as a period of depressed mood and/or loss of interest or pleasure in most activities, with other symptoms like change in body weight, constant sleep problems, tiredness, inability to think clearly, agitation, greatly slowed behaviour and thoughts of death and suicide. Other symptoms include excessive guilt or feelings of worthlessness.
- **Factors Predisposing Towards Depression** Genetic make-up or heredity, age, gender, negative life events and lack of social support are some important risk factors for major depression.
- **Mania** People suffering from mania become euphoric ('high'), extremely active, excessively talkative and easily distractible.

Bipolar Mood Disorder

- It is a mood disorder, in which both mania and depression are alternatively present, sometimes interrupted by periods of normal mood. Bipolar mood disorders were earlier referred to as manic-depressive disorders.
- Some types of bipolar and related disorders include 'Bipolar I Disorder', 'Bipolar II Disorder' and 'Cyclothymic Disorder'.

- An attempt of suicide is high in case of bipolar mood disorders. Several risk factors in addition to mental health status of a person predict the likelihood of suicide. Every suicide is a misfortune.
- To prevent suicide we need to identify vulnerability, comprehend the circumstances leading to such behaviour etc. Suicides are preventable. Some measures suggested by WHO are as follows
  - Limiting access to the means of suicide.
  - Reporting of suicide by media in a responsible way.
  - Bringing in alcohol related policies.
  - Early identification, treatment and care of people at risk.
  - Training health workers in assessing and managing for suicide.
  - Care for people who attempted suicide and providing community support.

Identifying Students in Distress

Some common factors are found in students who are in distress. These include, declining grades, decreasing effort, misbehaviour in the classroom, lack of interest in common activities, mysterious or repeated absence, smoking, drinking or drug misuse, etc.

Strengthening Student's Self-esteem

Some factors can enhance self-esteem of students. These are as follows

- **Positive life experiences** to develop positive identity which increases confidence in self.
- **Opportunities** are given to develop physical, social and vocational skills.
- Establish a **trustful communication**.
- **Goals** should be measurable, achievable which can be completed within specific time frame.

Schizophrenia Spectrum and Other Psychotic Disorders

Schizophrenia is the descriptive term for a group of psychotic disorders in which personal, social and occupational functioning deteriorate as a result of disturbed thought processes, strange perceptions, unusual emotional states and motor abnormalities. It is a **debilitating**[4] disorder. The social and psychological causes of schizophrenia are tremendous, both to patients as well as to their families and society.

Symptoms of Schizophrenia

The symptoms of schizophrenia can be grouped into three categories.

These are discussed as follows

1. Positive Symptoms

- These are 'pathological excesses' or 'bizarre (strange) additions' to a person's behaviour. Delusions, disorganised thinking and speech, heightened perception and hallucinations and inappropriate affects are some positive symptoms in schizophrenia.
- **Delusions** A delusion is a false belief that is firmly held on inadequate grounds. It has no basis in reality. People with delusion believe that they are being plotted against, slandered, threatened, attacked or deliberately victimised.

Mainly there are three types of delusions described as follows

  - (*i*) **Delusion of Reference** Schizophrenic people attach special and personal meaning to the actions of others or to objects and events.
  - (*ii*) **Delusion of Grandeur** Schizophrenic people believe themselves to be the specially empowered persons.
  - (*iii*) **Delusions to Control** Schizophrenic people believe that feeling, thoughts and actions are controlled by others.

- **Formal Thought Disorders** People with schizophrenia may not be able to think logically and may speak in strange ways. These formal thought disorders can make communication extremely difficult.
- These include rapidly shifting from one topic to another so that normal structure of thinking becomes illogical (loosening of associations, derailment), inventing new words or phrases (neologisms) and persistent and inappropriate repetition of the same thoughts (perseveration).
- **Hallucinations** Schizophrenic may have hallucinations. It is a perception that occurs in the absence of external stimuli. Auditory hallucinations are most common in schizophrenia. Patients hear sounds or voices that speak words, phrases and sentences directly to the patient (second-person hallucination) or talk to one another referring to the patient as she/he (third-person hallucination).

  Hallucinations can also involve the other senses. Some of these are as follows

  - Tactile hallucinations (i.e. forms of tingling, burning)
  - Somatic hallucinations (i.e. something happening inside the body such as a snake crawling inside one's stomach)
  - Visual hallucinations (i.e. unclear perceptions of colour or distinct visions of people or objects)
  - Gustatory hallucinations (i.e. food or drink taste becomes strange)
  - Olfactory hallucinations (i.e. smell of poison or smoke)

People with schizophrenia also show inappropriate affect, i.e. emotions that are unsuited to the situation.

---

4 Debilitating Making someone body or mind very weak.

2. Negative Symptoms

- These are 'pathological deficits' and include poverty of speech, **blunted affect**[5], flat affect, loss of volition (self determination) and social withdrawal.
- Patients with schizophrenia also experience avolition (lack of motivation or ability) and an inability to start or complete a course of action. People with this disorder may withdraw socially and become totally focussed on their own ideas and fantasies.

3. Psychomotor Symptoms

- People with schizophrenia show psychomotor symptoms i.e. they move less spontaneously or make odd grimaces (ugly expression with face) and gestures. These symptoms may take extreme forms known as **catatonia**. People in a catatonic stupor remain motionless and silent for long stretches of time.
- Some show catatonic rigidity i.e. maintaining a rigid, upright posture for hours while some others exhibit catatonic posturing i.e. assuming awkward, strange positions for long periods of time.

Neurodevelopmental Disorders

Neurodevelopmental disorders manifest in the early stage of development. Often these appears very early stage of childhood or during the early stage of schooling. These result in hampering personal, social, academic and occupational functioning.

Attention-Deficit Hyperactivity Disorder (ADHD)

Attention-deficit hyperactivity disorder is seen in children and demonstrate following features

Main features of ADHD are discussed below

- **Inattention** Children who are inattentive find it difficult to sustain mental effort during work or play. Some common complaints are that the child does not listen, cannot concentrate, does not follow instructions, is disorganised, easily distracted, forgetful, does not finish assignments and is quick to lose interest in boring activities.
- **Impulsivity** Children who are impulsive seem unable to control their immediate reactions or to think before they act. They find it difficult to wait or take turns, have difficulty in resisting immediate temptations or delaying them.
- **Hyperactivity** Children who are hyperactive are unable to control their motion. It is impossible for them to sit stable and quiet. The child may fidget, squirm (jiggle), climb and run around the room aimlessly. Boys are four times more likely to be given this diagnosis than girls.

Autism Spectrum Disorder

It is one of the most common of these disorders. Children with autistic disorder have marked difficulties in social interaction and communication, a restricted range of interests and strong desire for routine. Children with autism experience profound difficulties in relating to other people.

These difficulties are discussed as follows

- They are unable to initiate social behaviour and seem unresponsive to other people's feelings.
- They are unable to share experiences or emotions with others.
- They show serious abnormalities in communication and language that persist over time.
- Many autistic children never develop speech and those who do, have repetitive and deviant speech patterns.

Children with autism often show narrow patterns of interests and repetitive behaviours such as lining up objects or stereotyped body movements such as rocking.

These motor movements may be self-stimulatory such as hand flapping or self-injurious such as banging their head against the wall. People with autism tend to experience difficulties in starting, maintaining and even understanding relationships.

Intellectual Disability

Intellectual disability refers to below average intellectual functioning (an IQ of approximately 70 or below) and deficits in adaptive behaviour (i.e. in the areas of communication, self-care, home living, social/ interpersonal skills, functional academic skills, work, etc.) which are manifested before the age of 18 years.

---

5 Blunted affect It is a decreased ability to express emotion through your facial expressions (anger, sadness, joy, etc.)

Characteristics of Individuals with Different Levels of Intellectual Disability

Area of Functioning	Mild (IQ range = 55 to approximately 70)	Moderate (IQ range = 35-40 to approximately 50-55)	Severe (IQ range = 20-25 to approximately 35-40) and Profound (IQ = below 20-25)
Self-help Skills	Feeds and dresses self and cares for own toilet needs	Has difficulties and requires training but can learn adequate self-help skills	No skills to partial skills, but some can care for personal needs on limited; basis
Speech and Communication	Receptive and expressive language is adequate; understands communication	Receptive and expressive language is adequate; has speech problems	Receptive language is limited expressive language is poor
Academics	Optimal learning environment; third to sixth grade	Very few academic skills; first or second grade is maximal	No academic skills
Social Skills	Has friends; can learn to adjust quickly	Capable of making friends but has difficulty in many social situations	Not capable of having real friends; no social interactions
Vocational Adjustment	Can hold a job; competitive to semi-competitive; primarily unskilled work	Sheltered work environment; usually needs consistent supervision	Generally no employment; usually needs constant care
Adult Living	Usually marries, has children needs help during stress	Usually does not marry or have children; dependent	No marriage or children: always dependent on others

Specific Learning Disorder

In case of specific learning disorder, the individual experiences difficulty in perceiving or processing information correctly. During early school years students face problems in basic skills in reading, writing and mathematics. They perform poorly but with additional efforts can do better.

Disruptive, Impulse-Control and Conduct Disorders

The disorders included under this category are Oppositional Defiant Disorder (ODD), Conduct Disorders and Others. These are discussed as follows

Oppositional Defiant Disorder (ODD)

Children with Oppositional Defiant Disorder (ODD) are irritable, defiant, disobedient and behave in a hostile manner. Individuals with ODD do not see themselves as angry, oppositional and often justify their behaviour as reaction to circumstances/demands. Thus, the symptoms of the disorder become entangled with the problematic interactions with others. Unlike ADHD, the rates of ODD in boys and girls are not very different.

Conduct Disorder (CD) and Anti-social Behaviour

It refers to age inappropriate actions and attitudes that violate family expectations, societal norms and the personal or property rights of others. The behaviours in conduct disorder include aggressive actions that cause or threaten to harm people or animals, non-aggressive conduct that causes property damage, major deceitfulness or theft and serious rule violations.

Some types of aggressive behaviour are as follows

- Verbal aggression (i.e. name-calling, swearing)
- Physical aggression (i.e. hitting, fighting)
- Hostile aggression (i.e. directed at inflicting injury to others)
- Proactive aggression (i.e. dominating and bullying others without provocation).

Feeding and Eating Disorders

There are three types of eating disorders which are as follows

(i) **Anorexia Nervosa** In this, the individual has a disfigured body image that leads her/him to see herself/himself as overweight. By refusing to eat, exercising compulsively and developing unusual habits such as refusing to eat in front of others, the anorexic may lose large amounts of weight and even starve herself/himself to death.

(ii) **Bulimia Nervosa** In this, the individual may eat excessive amount of food, then clear her/his body of food by using medicines such as laxatives or diuretics or by vomiting. The person often feels disgusted and ashamed when she/he binges and is relieved of tension and negative emotions after purging.

(*iii*) **Binge Eating** In this, there are frequent episodes of out-of-control eating. In this case individual eats large amount of food, even if she/he is not feeling hungry. The patient tends to eat at a higher speed than normal and continues eating till she/he feels uncomfortably full.

Substance Related and Addictive Disorders

It involves excessive intake of high calorie food resulting in extreme obesity and the abuse of substances such as alcohol or cocaine. Disorders relating to maladaptive behaviours resulting from regular and consistent use of the substance involved are included under substance related and addictive disorders.

These disorders include problems associated with using and abusing drugs such as alcohol, cocaine and heroin. There are two sub-groups of substance-use disorders. These are as follows

(*i*) **Substance Dependence** In this, there is intense need to intake the substance to which the person is addicted and the person shows tolerance, withdrawal symptoms and compulsive drug-taking. Tolerance means that the person has to use more and more of a substance to get the same effect. Withdrawal refers to physical symptoms that occur when a person stops or cuts down on the use of a psychoactive substance. It means a substance that has the ability to change an individual's consciousness, mood and thinking processes.

(*ii*) **Substance Abuse** In this, there are recurrent and significant adverse consequences related to the use of substances. People who regularly ingest drugs damage their family and social relationships, perform poorly at work and create physical hazards.

The three most common forms of substance abuse are as follows

1. Alcohol Abuse and Dependence

People who abuse alcohol, drink large amount of alcohol regularly and rely on it to help them face difficult situations. The drinking interferes with social behaviour and ability to think and work.

For many people the pattern of alcohol abuse extends to dependence i.e. their bodies build up a tolerance for alcohol.

Some effects of alcohol abuse are as follows

- Alcoholism destroys millions of families, social relationships and careers. Intoxicated drivers are responsible for many road accidents.

- It also has serious effects on the children of persons with this disorder. These children have higher rates of psychological problems, particularly anxiety, depression, phobias and substance-related disorders.

- Excessive drinking can seriously damage physical health.

- All alcohol beverages contain ethyl alcohol. This chemical is absorbed into the blood and carried into the central nervous system (brain and spinal cord) where it depresses or slows down functioning.

- Ethyl alcohol depresses those areas in the brain that control judgement and inhibition; people become more talkative and friendly and they feel more confident and happy.

2. Heroin Abuse and Dependence

Heroin intake significantly interferes social and occupational functioning. Most abusers develop a dependence on heroin and experiencing a withdrawal reaction when they stop taking it.

The most direct danger of heroin abuse is an overdose, which slows down the respiratory centres in the brain, almost paralysing breathing and in many cases causing death.

3. Cocaine Abuse and Dependence

Regular use of cocaine may lead to a pattern of abuse in which the person may be intoxicated throughout the day and function poorly in social relationships and at work. It may also cause problems of short-term memory and attention.

In case of dependency, cocaine dominates the person's life as more drug is needed to get the desired effects and stopping it results in feelings of depression, fatigue, sleep problems, irritability and anxiety. Cocaine poses serious dangers. It has dangerous effects on psychological functioning and physical well-being.

Some Commonly Abused Substances

- Alcohol
- Stimulants (Dextroamphetamines, meta-amphetamines, cocaine)
- Caffeine (Coffee, tea, caffeinated soda, analgesics, chocolate, cocoa)
- Cannabis (marijuana or *bhang*, hashish, sensimilla)
- Hallucinogens (LSD (Lysergic Acid Diethylamide), mescaline)
- Inhalants (Gasoline, glue, paint thinners, spray paints, typewriter correction fluid, sprays)
- Tobacco (Cigarette, bidi)
- Opioid (morphine, heroin, cough syrup, painkillers-analgesics, anaesthetics)
- Sedatives, hypnotics or anxiolytics (Sleeping pills, anti-anxiety medication)

Chapter Practice

Objective Questions

• Multiple Choice Questions

1. Which of the following is not one of the four D of Psychological Disorder.
  (a) Deviant   (b) Depression
  (c) Distress   (d) Dangerous

Ans. (b) Depression is not the D of Psychological Disorder. The 4 Ds of psychological disorders are: Deviant, Distressing, Dysfunction and Danger.

2. ____ are stated or unstated rules of proper conduct.
  (a) Principles   (b) Manners
  (c) Norms   (d) Culture

Ans. (c) Norms are stated or unstated rules for proper conduct.

3. Which of the following current scheme of classification is used in India for psychological disorders?
  (a) ICD 10 classification of behavioural and mental disorders
  (b) ICD 11 classification of behavioural and mental disorders
  (c) ICD 10 classification of behavioural and psychological disorders
  (d) ICD 11 classification of behavioural and psychological disorders

Ans. (a) The current scheme of classification used in India for psychological disorders is the ICD-10 Classification of Behavioural and Mental Disorders. It was prepared by the World Health Organisation (WHO).

4. As per the ____ approach, abnormal psychology results when a person's brain and body do not work properly.
  (a) Psychological   (b) Organismic
  (c) Demonology   (d) Biological

Ans. (d) As per the biological approach, abnormal psychology results when a person's brain and body does not work properly.

5. In which mode of learning, behaviour is followed by a reward?
  (a) Classical conditioning
  (b) Operant conditioning
  (c) Social conditioning
  (d) All of the above

Ans. (b) In operant conditioning, the learning is often followed by a reward to promote the positive action or the required response.

6. Rakhi was travelling in a bus. She suddenly felt nervous. Her heart started beating very fast. She was sweating. This is an example of ________ .
  (a) Panic attack   (b) Heart attack
  (c) Bipolar disorder   (d) None of the above

Ans. (a) This is an example of panic attack. Panic Disorder frequent anxiety attacks characterised by feeling of intense terror.

7. Raj does not go to parks because he has a fear of dogs. This is an example of ________ .
  (a) Social phobia   (b) Specific phobia
  (c) Agoraphobia   (d) None of these

Ans. (b) This is an example of specific phobia. It is the most common phobia. This group includes irrational fears such as intense fear of a certain type of animal, or of being in an enclosed space.

8. What term is used when people develop a fear of entering unfamiliar situations?
  (a) Specific Phobia   (b) Social Phobia
  (c) Agoraphobia   (d) Astrophobia

Ans. (c) Agoraphobia is the term used when people develop a fear of entering unfamiliar situations. Many agoraphobics are afraid of leaving their homes.

9. After several years of living and working in a small town in Gujarat, Harsh wakes up one morning insisting that his name is Dhruv and that he has to report to his job in Mumbai. He does not recognise the furniture in his apartment or the clothing hanging in his closet. He is completely confused about his current life. He may be experiencing ________.
                        (CBSE Sample Paper 2020)

(a) Dissociative fugue
(b) Depersonalisation
(c) Generalised anxiety disorder
(d) Post-traumatic stress disorder

Ans. (a) Harsh may be experiencing Dissociative fugue.

10. __________ is the inability to stop over a particular idea.

(a) Aggressive behaviour   (b) Obsessive behaviour
(c) Depressed behaviour   (d) Introvert behaviour

Ans. (b) Obsessive behaviour is the inability to stop thinking about a particular idea or topic.

11. Dissociative amnesia is characterised by __________ .

1. extensive memory loss
2. non-selective memory loss
3. has no known organic cause
4. some patients might not remember anything from their past

Choose the correct option

(a) 1,2,3   (b) 2,3
(c) 1,3,4   (d) 2,4

Ans. (c) Dissociative amnesia is characterised by extensive but selective memory loss with no known organic cause. It may be caused by excessive stress. Some patients might not be able to remember anything from their past.

12. Bipolar disorder is characterised by the presence of both _____ and _____ alternatively.

(a) mania and depression
(b) happiness and sadness
(c) crying and laughing
(d) anger and empathy

Ans. (a) Bipolar disorder is characterised by the presence of both mania and depression alternatively.

13. Which of the following is not a feature of hyperactivity?

(a) It is more common in boys
(b) It is seen in children
(c) The child is shy and quite
(d) All of the above

Ans. (c) The child is shy and quite is not a feature of hyperactivity. Children who are hyperactive or who have attention deficit hyperactivity disorder often have problems in concentrate and paying attention. They are unable to sit quietly. The condition is four times more common in boys.

14. Cocaine abuse may cause problems in ___ memory.

(a) long-term   (b) short-term
(c) simple   (d) complex

Ans. (b) Cocaine abuse may cause problems in short-term memory. The long term memory remains unaffected.

15. Neha, a 17-year old girl, has been binging on large quantity of food, more than what most people of her age would eat. She, then, engages in purging behaviour as often as 3 or 4 times a week. She feels, as if, she has no control over it. She is most likely to be suffering from   **(CBSE Sample Paper 2020)**

(a) Anorexia Nervosa
(b) Bulimia Nervosa
(c) Binge Eating
(d) Eating disorder not otherwise specified

Ans. (b) Neha is most likely to be suffering from Bulimia Nervosa

Assertion and Reasoning

Directions (Q. Nos. 1-4) *Each of these questions contains two statements, Assertion (A) and Reason (R). Each of these question also has four alternative choices, any one of which is the correct answer. You have to select one of the codes (a), (b), (c) and (d) given below.*

(a) Both A and R are true and R is the correct explanation of A
(b) Both A and R are true, but R is not the correct explanation of A
(c) A is true, but R is false
(d) A is false, but R is true

1. **Assertion** (A) Abnormal behaviour is deviation from normal social norms.

Reasoning (R) Behaviours and ways of conduct that break society norms are thought to be abnormal.

Ans. (a) Abnormality refers to deviation from some clearly defined social norms or standards. Behaviours, thoughts and emotions that break the society norms are thought to be abnormal. Thus, both A and R are true and R is the correct explanation of A.

2. **Assertion** (A) Dissociative identity disorder is marked by a person having two or more identities.

Reasoning (R) This disorder often results from childhood trauma.

Ans. (a) Dissociative identity disorders is a condition in which a person may exhibit two or more identities with no knowledge of the multiple identity. This disorder is often reseults from childhood trauma or who may have gone through some stressful childhood events. The patient develops an alter ego that helps them bring out their subconscious instincts that they might have developed post a childhood traumatic incidence. Thus, both A and R are true and R is the correct explanation of A.

3. **Assertion** (A) Children with ADHD cannot sit still and are always distracted.

Reasoning (R) They have a deficiency of a growth factor.

Ans. (c) Children with Attention Deficit Hyperactivity Disorder or ADHD are hyper and cannot pay attention to a particular activity for a very long time. They have difficulty in sitting still and always distracted. The cause of ADHD is unknown. These kids are unable to control their actions. Boys are four times more likely to have ADHD compared to girls. Thus, A is true, but R is false.

4. **Assertion** (A) Anorexia nervosa is a tendency of a person to refuse food.

Reasoning (R) The person has a false image of his/her body shape.

Ans. (a) Anorexia nervosa is a psychological disorder in which a person often refuses to take food. In this disorder, the person develops false notions about his/ herself with various critical thoughts about their body. Hence, they start extensive dieting and exercising to reduce their weight to a level that is unhealthy. Thus, both A and R are true and R is the correct explanation of A.

• Case Based MCQs

1. Gary is a 19-year-old who withdrew from college after experiencing a manic episode during which he was brought to the attention of the Campus Police. He had changed his stream from engineering to philosophy. He spends his nights on phone, talking to his friends about life and reality. He had been convinced about the importance of his ideas, stating frequently that he was more learned and advanced than all his professors. He told others that he was on the verge of revolutionizing his new field, and he grew increasingly irritable and intolerant of anyone who disagreed with him. He also increased a number of high-risk behaviours – drinking and engaging in sexual relations in a way that was unlike his previous history. At the present time, he has returned home and has been placed on a mood stabilizer (after a period of time on an antipsychotic), and his psychiatrist is requesting adjunctive psychotherapy for his disorder. The patient's parents are somewhat shocked by the diagnosis, but they acknowledge that Gary had early problems with anxiety during pre-adolescence, followed by some periods of withdrawal and depression during his adolescence. His parents are eager to be involved in treatment, if appropriate.

(i) Identify the disorder with which Gary has been diagnosed?
(a) Panic Disorder
(b) Bipolar Disorder
(c) Schizophrenia
(d) Social Anxiety Disorder

Ans. (b) Gary has been diagnosed with Bipolar disorder which is characterised by episodes of both mania and depression with phases of stability in between the episodes.

(ii) Another term that has been previously used for bipolar disorder is __________ .
(a) Schizophrenia
(b) Paranoid schizophrenia
(c) Manic-depressive disorder
(d) Multiple personality disorder

Ans. (c) Previously the term used for biopolar disorder is manic-depressive disorder.

(iii) Bipolar disorder is what type of disorder?
(a) Personality   (b) Mood
(c) Identity   (d) Thought

Ans. (b) Bipolar disorder is a type of mood disorder dealing with mania and depression.

(iv) In case of Gary, the manic episodes were followed by __________ .
(a) Depressive episodes   (b) Crime sprees
(c) Lying   (d) Sleepwalking

Ans. (b) In case of Gary, the manic episodes soon took a form of crime sprees.

(v) **Assertion** (A) A high rate of suicide has been noted with patients of bipolar disorder.

Reason (R) It is a result of a complex interface of biological, genetic, psychological, sociological, cultural and environmental factors.

Codes
(a) Both A and R are true and R is the correct explanation of A
(b) Both A and R are true, but R is not the correct explanation of A
(c) A is true, but R is false
(d) R is true, but A is false

Ans. (a) Bipolar disorder has shown a high risk of suicide. Suicidal behaviour indicates difficulties in problem solving, stress management and emotional expression. It is a result of a complex interface of biological, genetic, psychological, sociological and environmental factors. Thus, both A and R are true and R is the correct explanation of A.

(vi) WHO has been working hard to bring down the rate of suicide in psychological patients. Which of the following techniques have been used by WHO for this purpose?
(a) Limiting access to the means of suicide
(b) Reporting of suicide by media in a responsible way
(c) Bringing in alcohol related policies
(d) All of the above

Ans. (d) All of above are the techniques used by WHO for this purpose.

Subjective Questions

• Short Answer (SA) Type Questions

1. What are the various approaches used to distinguish between normal and abnormal behaviour?

Ans. Various approaches have been used to distinguish between normal and abnormal behaviours. From these approaches, two basic and conflicting views emerged which are as follows

   (i) The first approach refers to abnormal behaviour as a deviation from the social norms. Each society has norms, which are stated or unstated rules for proper conduct. Behaviours, thoughts and emotions that break societal norms are called **abnormal**.

   A society's norms grow from its particular culture. Culture includes history, values, institutions, habits, skills, technology and arts.

   A society's values may change over time. It is based on the assumption that socially accepted behaviour is not abnormal, and that normality is nothing more than conformity to social norms.

   (ii) The second approach views abnormal behaviour as maladaptive. Many psychologists think that the normality of behaviour does not depend on the fact whether society accepts it or not, but it depends on the well-being of the individual and group. Well-being is not only maintenance or survival, but it includes growth and fulfillment.

2. Describe the role of biological factors in abnormal behaviour.

Ans. The role of biological factors in abnormal behaviour is given below

   • Biological factors influence all aspects of our behaviour. A wide range of these factors such as faulty genes, endocrine imbalances, malnutrition, injuries and other conditions may interfere with normal development and functioning of the human body.

   • Biological factors like psychological disorders are related to problems in the transmission of messages from one neuron to another.

   • When an electrical impulse reaches a neuron's ending, the nerve ending is stimulated to release a chemical, called a neurotransmitter.

   • Some other biological factors like Anxiety disorders have been linked to low activity of the neurotransmitter Gamma Amino Butyric Acid (GABA). Similarly, schizophrenia have been linked to excess activity of dopamine, and depression have been linked to low activity of serotonin.

3. Explain mental disorders from a cognitive perspective. **(CBSE 2018)**

Ans. Mental disorder is a deviation from social norm. Each society has norms which are stated or unstated rules for proper conduct. Behaviour, thoughts and emotions that break societal norms are called abnormal behaviour.

To explain mental disorders there are several psychological models. These models maintain that psychological and interpersonal factors have a significant role to play in abnormal behaviour. This psychological models include cognitive model. Psychological factors are emphasised by the cognitive model.

This model states that abnormal functioning can result from cognitive problems. People may hold assumptions and attitudes about themselves that are irrational and inaccurate. They may also repeatedly think in illogical ways. Sometimes, they make overgeneralisations and draw broad, negative conclusions on the basis of a single insignificant event.

4. Describe socio-cultural model of abnormal behaviour. **(Delhi 2015, 2016)**

Or Explain mental disorder from socio-cultural perspective.

Ans. The socio-cultural model of abnormal behaviour means social and cultural forces that influence an individual. As behaviour is shaped by societal, factors such as family structure and communication, social networks, societal conditions, and societal labels and roles become more important.

It has been found that certain family systems are likely to produce abnormal functioning in individual members. Some families have a structure in which the members are overinvolved in each other's activities, thoughts, and feelings. Children from this kind of family may have difficulty in becoming independent in life.

The broader social networks in which people operate include their social and professional relationships. Studies have shown that people who are isolated and lack social support i.e. strong and fulfilling interpersonal relationships in their lives, are likely to become more depressed and remain depressed longer than those who have good friendships.

5. Discuss briefly diathesis-stress model.

Ans. This model states that psychological disorders develop when a diathesis (biological pre-disposition to the disorder) is set off by a stressful situation. This model has three components. These are as follows

   (i) The first component is the diathesis or the presence of some biological disorders which may be inherited.

(ii) The second component is that the diathesis may carry a vulnerability to develop a psychological disorder. This means that the person is 'at risk' or 'predisposed' to develop the disorder.

(iii) The third component is the presence of pathogenic stressors i.e. factors/stressors that may lead to psychopathology.

This model has been applied to several disorders including anxiety, depression, and schizophrenia.

6. What is obsessive-compulsive disorder? Explain. **(Delhi 2017)**

Ans. Obsessive behaviour is the inability to stop thinking about a particular idea or topic. Compulsive behaviour is the need to perform certain behaviours over and over again. Many compulsions deal with counting, ordering, checking, touching and washing. People affected by obsessive-compulsive disorder are unable to control their preoccupation with specific ideas or are unable to prevent themselves from repeatedly carrying out a particular act or series of acts that affect their ability to carry out normal activities.

7. Can a distorted body image lead to eating disorders? Classify the various forms of it. **(NCERT)**

Ans. A distorted body image lead to eating disorders. There are three types of eating disorders which are as follows

(i) **Anorexia Nervosa** In this, the individual has a disfigured body image that leads her/ him to see herself/himself as overweight. By refusing to eat, exercising compulsively and developing unusual habits such as refusing to eat in front of others, the anorexic may lose large amount of weight and even starve herself/himself to death.

(ii) **Bulimia Nervosa** In this, the individual may eat excessive amount of food, then clear her/his body of food by using medicines such as laxatives or diuretics or by vomiting. The person often feels disgusted and ashamed when she/he binges and is relieved of tension and negative emotions after purging.

(iii) **Binge Eating** In this, there are frequent episodes of out-of-control eating. The individual eats at a high speed than normal and takes a large amount of food even when he is not feeling hungry.

8. What are dissociative disorders. Explain their various types. **(CBSE 2019)**

Ans. Dissociation disorder involves feeling of unreality, estrangement, depersonalisation and sometimes a loss or shift of identity. Four conditions are included in this disorder. These are as follows

(i) **Dissociative Amnesia** It is characterised by extensive or selective memory loss that has no known organic cause. This order is often associated with an overwhelming stress.

(ii) **Dissociative Fugue** is characterised as the assumption of a new identity and the inability to recall the previous identity.

(iii) **Dissociative Identity Disorder** is referred to as multiple personality disorder and is the most dramatic of the dissociative disorders.

(iv) **Depersonalisation** involves an imaginary state in which the person has a sense of being separated both from self and from reality.

9. Identify the symptoms associated with depression and mania. **(NCERT)**

Ans. Depression and Mania are mood descenders.

Depression It covers a variety of negative moods and behavioural changes. People suffering from depression associated with following symptoms

- change in body weight
- constant sleep problems
- tiredness
- inability to think clearly
- agitation
- negative sely-concept
- no interest in pleasurable activities
- greatly slowed behaviour
- thoughts of death and suicide

Mania People suffering from mania associated with following symptoms

- become euphoric (high)
- extremely active
- excessively talkative
- easily distractible

10. What is bipolar mood disorder? **(CBSE 2016)**

Ans. Bipolar mood disorder is a mental illness that causes dramatic changes in the person's mood, energy and ability to think clearly. People with bipolar mood diorder experience high and low moods which are known as mania and depression.

Some types of bipolar and related disorders include 'Bipolar I Disorder', 'Bipolar II Disorder' and 'Cyclothymic Disorder'.

An attempt of suicide is high in case of Bipolar disorder. There are several risk factors in addition to mental health status of a person predict the likelihood of suicide. These include

- Age
- Gender
- Ethnicity
- Race
- Recent occurrence of serious life events.

11. Differentiate between delusions and hallucinations.
(Delhi 2016)

Ans. The difference between delusions and hallucinations are as follows

Delusion	Hallucination
Delusion is a false belief, that is firmly held on inadequate grounds.	It is a perception that occurs in the absence of external stimuli.
Delusions can be about people or things.	Hallucinations are very real to the person experiencing them.
Patients with delusion believe that they are being plotted against, threatened, attacked or deliberately victimized.	In Hallucination patients hear sounds or voices that speak words phrases, sentences directly to the patients.
Medical conditions that can cause delusions are obsessive compulsive disorder, Epilepsy. Al zheimer's disease, etc.	Medical condition that can cause hallucination are lack of sleep, mental illness, social isolation, etc.

12. What is autistic disorder? Also explain the difficulties faced by the children suffer with autistic disorder.

Ans. Autistic disorder or autism is one of the most common disorders among children. Children with autistic disorder have marked difficulties in social interaction and communication, a restricted range of interests, and strong desire for routine. Children with autism experience profound difficulties in relating to other people.

These difficulties are as follows

- They are unable to initiate social behaviour and seem unresponsive to other people's feelings.
- They are unable to share experiences or emotions with others.
- They show serious abnormalities in communication and language that persist over time.
- Many autistic children never develop speech and those who do, have repetitive and deviant speech patterns.
- Children with autism often show narrow patterns of interests and repetitive behaviours such as lining up objects or stereotyped body movements such as rocking. These motor movements may be self-stimulatory such as hand flapping or self-injurious such as banging their head against the wall.

13. Explain disruptive, impulse-control and conduct disorders. (CBSE 2019)

Ans. Disruptive, impulse-control and conduct disorders refer to a group of diorders that include oppositional defiant disorder, conduct disorder and anti-social behaviour which are discussed as follows

- **Oppositional Defiant Disorder** (ODD) Children with Oppositional Defiant Disorder (ODD) are irritable, defiant, disobedient and behave in a hostile manner.

However, they do not see themselves as angry, oppositional or defiant. They often justify their behaviour as reaction to circumstances or demands. So, the symptom of the disorder become entangled with the problematic interactions with others.

- **Conduct Disorder (CD) and Anti-social Behaviour** It refers to age inappropriate actions and attitudes that violate family expectations, societal norms and the personal or property rights of others. The behaviours in conduct disorder include aggressive actions that cause threaten and harm to people or animals, non-aggressive conduct that causes property damage, major deceitfulness or theft and serious rule violations.

14. Raj would often be seen talking to himself. On questioning, he would state that there were people around him whom he could see and hear when there was no one else around. Identify and describe this symptom of schizophrenia.

Ans. People with schizophrenia may have hallucinations, i.e. perceptions that occur in the absence of external stimuli. Auditory hallucinations are most common in schizophrenia. Patients hear sounds or voices that speak words, phrases and sentences directly to the patient (second-person hallucination) or talk to one another referring to the patient as s/he (third person hallucination). Hallucinations can also involve the other senses. These include tactile hallucinations (i.e. forms of tingling, burning), somatic hallucinations (i.e. something happening inside the body such as a snake crawling inside one's stomach), visual hallucinations (i.e. vague perceptions of colour or distinct visions of people or objects), gustatory hallucinations (i.e. food or drink taste strange), and olfactory hallucinations (i.e. smell of poison or smoke).

15. Aman is an eight year old who has profound difficulty in relating to other people. Often, he is found to be unresponsive to other people's feelings and exhibits stereotypical patterns of behaviour. Identify this disorder and describe its features.

Ans. Children with autism spectrum disorder experience profound difficulties in relating to other people. They are unable to initiate social behaviour and seem unresponsive to other people's feelings. They are unable to share experiences or emotions with others. They also show serious abnormalities in communication and language that persist over time. Many of them never develop speech and those who do, have repetitive and deviant speech patterns. Such children often show narrow patterns of interests and repetitive behaviours such as lining up objects or stereotyped body movements such as rocking. These motor movements may be self-stimulatory such as hand flapping or self-injurious such as banging their head against the wall. Due to the nature of these difficulties in terms of verbal and non-verbal communication, individuals with autism spectrum disorder tend to experience difficulties in starting, maintaining and even understanding relationships.

16. What are phobias? If someone had an intense fear of snakes, could this simple phobia be a result of faulty learning? Analyse how this phobia could have developed. **(NCERT)**

Ans. **Phobias** It refers to irrational fears related to specific objects, interactions with others, and unfamiliar situations. If someone had an intense fear of snakes, this simple phobia cannot be a result of faulty learning. It is a specific phobia which is most common. This group includes irrational fears such as intense fear of a certain type of animal, or of being in an enclosed space.

This phobia often develops gradually or begins with a generalised anxiety disorders. The symptoms include worry and apprehensive feelings about the future and hypervigilance, which involves constantly scanning the environment for dangers.

It is marked by motor tension, as a result of which the person is unable to relax, is restless, and visibly shaky (weak) and tense.

17. Distinguish between obsessions and compulsions. **(NCERT)**

Ans. The difference between obsessions and compulsions are as follows

Obsessions	Compulsions
They are thoughts, ideas and impulses.	They are actions.
They cause unwanted feelings, anxiety and distress.	They are performed to cope with obsessions.
They lead to compulsions, (cause)	They result due to obsessions. (Effect).
They disrupt the mental wellbeing.	They disrupt the physical wellbeing.

• Long Answer (LA) Type Questions

1. Describe the psychological models to explain abnormal behaviour/mental disorders.
(CBSE 2019, Delhi 2014)

Ans. The psychological and interpersonal factors have a significant role to play in abnormal behaviour.

The psychological models include the following

(i) **Psychodynamic Model** It is the oldest and most famous of the modern psychological models. Psychodynamic theorists believe that behaviour, whether normal or abnormal is determined by psychological forces within the person of which she/he is not consciously aware.

(ii) **Behavioural Model** This model states that both normal and abnormal behaviours are learned and psychological disorders are the result of learning maladaptive ways of behaving.

(iii) **Cognitive Model** This model states that abnormal functioning can result from cognitive problems. People may hold assumptions and attitudes about themselves that are irrational and inaccurate.

(iv) **Humanistic-Existential Model** It focuses on broader aspects of human existence. Humanists believe that human beings are born with a natural tendency to be friendly, cooperative and constructive and are driven to self-actualise i.e., to fulfil this potential for goodness and growth.

(v) **Socio-Cultural Model** According to the socio-cultural model, abnormal behaviour is best understood by the social and cultural forces that influence an individual.

(vi) **Diathesis-Stress Model** This model states that psychological disorders develop when a diathesis (biological pre-disposition to the disorder) is set off by a stressful situation.

2. Can a long-standing pattern of deviant behaviour be considered abnormal? Elaborate. **(NCERT)**

Ans. Yes, a long standing pattern of deviant behaviour is considered to be abnormal. The word 'abnormal' literally means 'away from the normal'. It implies deviation from some clearly defined norms or standards. In psychology, we have no 'ideal model' or 'normal model' of human behaviour to use as a base for comparison. Various approaches have been used in distinguishing between normal and abnormal behaviours.

From these approaches, two basic and conflicting views emerged

(i) The first approach views abnormal behaviour as a deviation from social norms. Abnormal behaviour, thoughts and emotions are different from a society's ideas of proper functioning.

A society that values competition and assertiveness may accept aggressive behaviour, whereas one that emphasises cooperation and family values (such as in India) may consider aggressive behaviour as unacceptable or even abnormal.

(ii) The second approach views abnormal behaviour as maladaptive. The best criterion for determining the normality of behaviour is whether society promotes the well-being of the individual and i.e. the group to which she/he belongs.

Well-being is not simply a maintenance and survival but also includes growth and fulfilment i.e. the actualisation of potential. According to this criterion, conforming behaviour can be seen as abnormal if it is maladaptive i.e., if it interferes with optimal functioning and growth.

3. Explain abnormality. Trace a brief history of how our understanding of psychological disorders has evolved to its current status. **(CBSE 2019)**

Ans. The word 'abnormal' literally means 'away from the normal'. It implies deviation from some clearly defined norms or standards.

In Ancient times, abnormality holds that abnormal behaviour can be explained by the operation of supernatural and magical forces such as evil spirits (*bhoot-pret*) or the devil (*shaitan*).

Exorcism i.e. removing the evil that resides in the individual through countermagic and prayer is still commonly used. In many societies, the *shaman* or medicine man (*ojha*) is a person who is believed to have contact with supernatural forces and is the medium through which spirits communicate with human beings.

It is believed that through *shaman*, an affected person can know which spirit is responsible for his problem and what needs to be done to appease the spirit.

In Renaissance period Johann Weyer emphasised psychological conflict and disturbed interpersonal relationship as causes of psychological disorder. The growth of scientific attitude toward psychological disorder developed in the 18th century as a result of Reform Movement.

It provided community care for mentally ill person. In recent years, it is believed that biological, psychological and social factors play important roles in influencing the expression and outcome of psychological disorders.

4. Describe the symptoms of any two anxiety disorders. **(CBSE 2020)**

Or Classify and explain the symptoms of eating disorders. **(CBSE 2020)**

Ans. One of the major psychological disorders is anxiety disorder. The term anxiety is defined as a diffuse, vague, very unpleasant feeling of fear and apprehension. The mental disorder which arises due to anxiety is known as anxiety disorder.

Two main types of anxiety disorders are as follows

Generalised Anxiety Disorder It consists of continued, vague (unclear), unexplained and intense fears that are not attached to any particular object. The symptoms include worry and apprehensive feelings about the future; hypervigilance, which involves constantly scanning the environment for dangers.

It is marked by motor tension, as a result of which the person is unable to relax, is restless and visibly shaky (weak) and tense.

Panic Disorder It consists of recurrent anxiety attacks in which the person experiences intense terror. A panic attack denotes an abrupt rise of intense anxiety rising to

a peak when thoughts of a particular stimuli are present. Such thoughts occur in an unpredictable manner. The Clinical features include, Shortness of breath, Dizziness, Trembling, Palpitations, Choking, Nausea, Chest pain or discomfort, Fear of going crazy, Losing control, dying.

Or There are three types of eating disorders. These are discussed as follows

  (i) **Anorexia Nervosa** In this, the individual has a disfigured body image that leads her/him to see herself/himself as overweight. By refusing to eat, exercising compulsively and developing unusual habits such as refusing to eat in front of others, the anorexic may lose large amounts of weight and even starve herself/himself to death.

  (ii) **Bulimia Nervosa** In this, the individual may eat excessive amount of food, then clear her/his body of food by using medicines such as laxatives or diuretics or by vomiting. The person often feels disgusted and ashamed when she/he binges and is relieved of tension and negative emotions after purging.

  (iii) **Binge Eating** In this, there are frequent episodes of elaborad out-of-control eating. In this case individual eats large amount of food, even he is not feeling hungry. He tends to eat at a higher speed than normal and continues eating till he feels uncomfortably full.

5. What do you understand by the term 'dissociation'? Explain the types of dissociative disorder. **(All India 2016)**

Or What do you understand by the term 'dissociation'? Discuss its various forms. **(NCERT)**

Ans. Dissociation involves feelings of unreality, estrangement, depersonalisation, and sometimes a loss or shift of identity. Sudden temporary alterations of consciousness that blot out painful experiences are a defining characteristic of dissociative disorders.

There are four types of dissociation. These are as follows

  (i) **Dissociative Amnesia** It is characterised by extensive but selective memory loss that has no known organic cause (e.g., head injury) in which some people cannot remember anything about their past. Others are no longer recall specific events, peoples, places or objects while their memory for other events remain intact. This disorder is often associated with an overwhelming stress.

  (ii) **Dissociative Fugue** It characterises the assumption of a new identity, and the inability to recall the previous identity. Unexpected travel away from home or workplace.

  (iii) **Dissociative Identity Disorder** It is often referred to as multiple personality disorder and is the most dramatic of the dissociative disorders. It is often associated with traumatic experiences in childhood.

(iv) **Depersonalisation** It involves an imaginary state in which the person has a sense of being separated both from self and from reality. In depersonalisation, there is a change of self-perception. The person's sense of reality is temporarily lost or changed.

6. What is depression? Discuss the main types of mood disorders.

Ans. The most common mood disorder is depression. Depression covers a variety of negative moods and behavioural changes.

We often use the term depression to refer to normal feelings after a significant loss, such as the break-up of a relationship or the failure to attain a significant goal.

Genetic make-up or heredity, age, gender, negative life events and lack of social support are some important risk factors for major depression.

Major Depressive Disorder It is defined as a period of depressed mood and/or loss of interest or pleasure in most activities, with other symptoms like change in body weight, constant sleep problems, tiredness, inability to think clearly, agitation, greatly slowed behaviour and thoughts of death and suicide. Other symptoms include excessive guilt or feelings of worthlessness.

Mania People suffering from mania become euphoric ('high'), extremely active, excessively talkative and easily distractible.

Bipolar is a mood disorder, in which both mania and depression are alternately present, is sometimes interrupted by periods of normal mood. Bipolar mood disorders were earlier referred to as manic-depressive disorders.

Some types of bipolar and related disorders include 'Bipolar I Disorder', 'Bipolar II Disorder' and 'Cyclothymic Disorder'. Among the mood disorders, the lifetime risk of a suicide attempt is high in case of bipolar mood disorders.

Suicide Several risk factors in addition to mental health status of a person predict the likelihood of suicide. Every suicide is a misfortune.

7. Explain the main featuers of ADSD.

Or Describe the characteristics of hyperactive children.   **(NCERT)**

Ans. The main features of ADHD are as follows

- **Inattention** Children who are inattentive find it difficult to sustain mental effort during work or play. Some common complaints are that the child does not listen, cannot concentrate, does not follow instructions, is disorganised, easily distracted, forgetful, does not finish assignments, and is quick to lose interest in boring activities.

- **Impulsivity** Children who are impulsive seem unable to control their immediate reactions or to think before they act. They find it difficult to wait or take turns, have difficulty in resisting immediate temptations or delaying gratification.

- **Hyperactivity** Children who are hyperactive are unable to control their motion. It is impossible for them to sit stable and quiet. The child may fidget, squirm (jiggle), climb and run around the room aimlessly. Boys are four times more likely to be given this diagnosis than girls.

The characteristics of hyperactive children are as follows

- Children who are hyperactive seen unable to control their motion.

- It is impossible for them to sit stable and quiet.

- The child may fidget, squirm, climb and run around the room aimlessly.

- Boys are four times more likely to be given this diagnosis than girls.

8. While speaking in public the patient changes topics frequently, is this a positive or a negative symptom of schizophrenia? Describe the other symptoms and sub-types of schizophrenia.   **(NCERT)**

Ans. It is a formal thought disorder which is a positive symptom of **schizophrenia**. People with schizophrenia may not be able to think logically and may speak in peculiar ways. People rapidly shift from one topic to another so that the normal structure of thinking is muddled and becomes illogical.

The symptoms of schizophrenia can be grouped into three categories

(i) **Positive symptoms** These are pathological excesses or bizarre (strange) additions to a person's behaviour. Delusions, disorganised thinking and speech, heightened perception and hallucinations and inappropriate affect are some symptoms in schizophrenia. These are discussed as follows

 (a) **Delusions** A delusion is a false belief that is firmly held on inadequate grounds. It is not affected by rational argument, and has no basis in reality.

 (b) **Formal Thought Disorders** People with schizophrenia may not be able to think logically and may speak in strange ways. These formal thought disorders can make communication extremely difficult.

 (c) **Hallucinations** It is a perception that occurs in the absence of external stimuli. Auditory hallucinations are most common in schizophrenia.

(ii) **Negative Symptoms** These are pathological deficits and include poverty of speech, blunted (weakened) and flat affect, loss of volition (self determination) and social withdrawal. People with schizophrenia show alogia or poverty of speech i.e., a reduction in speech and speech content.

(iii) **Psychomotor Symptoms** People with schizophrenia show psychomotor symptoms i.e.
  - They move less spontaneously or make odd grimaces and gestures.
  - These symptoms may take extreme forms known as catatonia.
  - People in a catatonic stupor remain motionless and silent for long stretches of time.
  - Some show catatonic rigidity i.e., maintaining a rigid, upright posture for hours while some others exhibit catatonic posturing i.e., assuming awkward, strange positions for long periods.

9. Anxiety has been called the "butterflies in the stomach feeling". At what stage does anxiety become a disorder? Discuss its types. **(NCERT)**

Ans. The term anxiety is usually defined as a diffuse, vague, very unpleasant feeling of fear and apprehension. Hence, it is called "butterflies in the stomach feeling".

When an individual shows the symptoms the combination with anxiety on that stage anxiety becames an disorder.

The anxious individual shows the following symptoms
  - Rapid heart rate
  - Diarrhoea
  - Fainting
  - Sweating
  - Frequent urination
  - Shortness of breath
  - Loss of appetite
  - Dizziness
  - Sleeplessness
  - Tremors

Types of anxiety disorders are as follows

Generalised Anxiety Disorder It consists of prolonged, vague, unexplained and intense fears that are not attached to any particular object.

The symptoms include worry and apprehensive feelings about the future; hypervigilance, which involves constantly scanning the environment for dangers.

Panic Disorder It consists of recurrent anxiety attacks in which the person experiences intense terror. A panic attack denotes an abrupt surge (rise) of intense anxiety rising to a peak when thoughts of a particular stimuli are present.

Phobia People who have phobias have irrational fears related to specific objects, people, or situations. Phobias can be grouped into three main types, i.e. specific phobias, social phobias, and agoraphobia.

 (i) **Specific Phobia** This group includes irrational fears such as intense fear of a certain type of animal, or of being in an enclosed space.

 (ii) **Social Phobia** Intense and incapacitating fear and embarrassment when dealing with others characterises social phobias.

 (iii) **Agoraphobia** It is the term used when people develop a fear of entering unfamiliar situations.

Obsessive-Compulsive Disorder People affected by obsessive-compulsive disorder are unable to control their preoccupation with specific ideas or are unable to prevent themselves from repeatedly carrying out a particular act or series of acts that affect their ability to carry out normal activities. Obsessive behaviour is the inability to stop thinking about a particular idea or topic.

Compulsive behaviour is the need to perform certain behaviours over and over again. Many compulsions deal with counting, ordering, checking, touching and washing.

Post-Traumatic Stress Disorder (PTSD) People who have been caught in a natural disaster (such as tsunami) or have been victims of bomb blasts by terrorists, or been in a serious accident or in a war-related situation, experience Post-Traumatic Stress Disorder (PTSD).

● Case Based Questions

1. Schizophrenia is the descriptive term for a group of psychotic disorders in which personal, social and occupational functioning deteriorate as a result of disturbed thought processes, strange perceptions, unusual emotional states, and motor abnormalities. It is a debilitating disorder.

The social and psychological costs of schizophrenia are tremendous, both to patients as well as to their families and society

Symptoms of schizophrenia can be classified as Positive symptoms (i.e. excesses of thought, emotion, and behaviour), negative symptoms (i.e. deficits of thought, emotion, and behaviour), and psychomotor symptoms.

 (i) What are delusions? Explain different types of delusions seen in schizophrenia.

Ans. A delusion is a false belief that is firmly held on inadequate grounds. It is not affected by rational argument, and has no basis in reality.

There are mainly three types of delusion seen in schizophrenia. These are as follows

  - **Delusions of reference** In this type of delusion, people attach special and personal meaning to the actions of others or to objects and events.
  - **Delusions of grandeur** In this type of delusion, people believe themselves to be specially empowered persons.
  - **Delusions of control,** Schizophrenic people believe that their feelings, thoughts and actions are controlled by others.

 (ii) Explain different types of hallucinations.

Ans. Schizophrenics may have hallucinations, i.e. perceptions that occur in the absence of external stimuli.

Some of the different types of hallucinations that exist are as follows

Auditory hallucinations These are false perceptions of sound. It is one of the most prevalent symptoms of schizophrenia.

(iii) What is catatonia? Explain its role in schizophrenia.

Ans. People with schizophrenia also show psychomotor symptoms. They move less spontaneously or make odd grimaces and gestures. These symptoms may take extreme forms known as catatonia. People in a catatonic stupor remain motionless and silent for long stretches of time. Some show catatonic rigidity, i.e. maintaining a rigid, upright posture for hours. Others exhibit catatonic posturing, i.e. assuming awkward, bizarre positions for long periods of time.

2. Sunny is a 7 year old boy. His parents are worried about his lack of paying attention in the class. As per his teacher, Sunny is highly distracted during the lesson and keeps looking here and there. He cannot sit steady and keeps talking to his partner.

When asked, Sunny's mother said that he has always been over active and is unable to focus on a particular task for a very long time.

Sunny's school performance was always below average and has only been deteriorating. Sunny was diagnosed with attention deficit hyperactivity disorder ADHD and has been going through therapy.

(i) What are the symptoms of ADHD that helps to identify the disorder?

Ans. The main symptoms of ADHD that helps in identifying disorder are Inattentive, Hyeractive and Impulsive. A person with ADHD struggles harder in paying attention, listen, follow direction, etc.

(ii) What is impulsivity? Explain.

Ans. Impulsivity is the tendency to act without thinking. Children who are impulsive find it difficult to wait his turn. For eg. Run across the strect without looking, buy something without any plan, etc.

(iii) What is hyperactivity? What are the characteristics of a hyperactivity?

Ans. Hyperactivity is a state of being unusually or abnormally active. The child who shows a pattern of hyperactive may fidgel, squirm, climb and run around the room aimlessly.

Tactile Hallucination This refers to the feelings of movement or sensation on body that are not actually present.

Visual Hallucination This refers to a condition in which a person sees something that does not exist or sees something that does exist but sees it incorrectly.

3. Addictive behaviour, whether it involves excessive intake of high calorie food resulting in extreme obesity or involving the abuse of substances such as alcohol or cocaine, is one of the most severe problems being faced by society today. Disorders relating to maladaptive behaviours resulting from regular and consistent use of the substance involved are called substance abuse disorders. These disorders include problems associated with using and abusing such as drugs, alcohol, cocaine and heroin, which alter the way people think, feel and behave. There are two sub-groups of substance-use disorders, i.e. those related to substance dependence and those related to substance abuse. We will now focus on the three most common forms of substance abuse, viz. alcohol abuse and dependence, heroin abuse and dependence, and cocaine abuse and dependence.

(i) What is alcoholism? What are the signs of alcohol abuse?

Ans. Alcoholism is a condition when a person's drinking habit interferes with his/her work and social life. There are many signs of alcohol abuse. Some of them are as follows

- People who abuse alcohol, drink large amount regularly.
- They rely on alcohol to help them face stressful situations.
- Alcohol interferes with their social behaviour.
- It also interferes with the ability to think and work.
- Dependence on alcohol develops rapidly.

(ii) Write about some commonly abused substances.

Ans.
- Alcohol
  - Amphetamines: dextroamphetamines, methamphetamines, diet pills
  - Caffeine: coffee, tea, caffeinated soda, analgesics, chocolate, cocoa
  - Cannabis: marijuana or 'bhang', hashish, sensimilla
  - Cocaine
  - Hallucinogens: LSD, mescaline
  - Inhalants: gasoline, glue, paint thinners, spray paints, typewriter correction fluid, sprays
  - Nicotine: cigarettes, tobacco
  - Phencyclidine
  - Sedatives

(iii) Write a short note on Heroin abuse.

Ans. Heroin intake significantly interferes with social and occupational functioning. Most abusers further develop a dependence on heroin. Patients often develop a tolerance for it, and experiencing a withdrawal reaction when they stop taking it. The most direct withdrawal symptoms are feelings of depression, fatigue, sleep problems, irritability and anxiety.

Chapter Test

Multiple choice questions

1. Alogia means
   - (a) Sponge taste of drink
   - (b) Poverty of speech
   - (c) Smell of poison
   - (d) None of these

2. Which of the following is an opioid?
   - (a) Morphine
   - (b) Heroin
   - (c) Cough syrup
   - (d) All of these

3. Which of the following contains nicotine?
   - (a) Tobacco
   - (b) Bhang
   - (c) Coffee
   - (d) Heroin

4. One day during his lunch hour, Geraldo suddenly could not breathe. He felt his heart racing, he began to hyperventilate, and he became worried that he was dying. He wanted to get help from his coworkers, but he was worried about embarrassing himself in front of them. If these episodes continue, then Geraldo might be diagnosed with _______.
   - (a) bipolar disorder
   - (b) panic disorder
   - (c) generalized anxiety disorder
   - (d) simple phobia

Short Answer Type Questions

5. Discuss conduct disorder.

6. Briefly discuss anorexia nervosa.

7. Describe in brief the sub types of schizophrenia.

8. Explain diathesis-stress model.

9. Describe biological and genetic factors responsible for abnormal behaviour.

10. Shalini often eat excessive amounts of food, then purge her body of food by using medicines such as laxatives or diuretics or by vomiting. Identify the psychological disorder that Shalini may have? Also, Give reason why she might be doing so?

Long Answer Type Questions

11. Elaborate major anxiety disorders and their symptoms.

12. Elaborate the symptoms of schizophrenia.

13. Explain various effects of alcohol.

14. A psychologist while diagnosing the patient has concluded that the psychological disorder of patient can be attributed to biochemical or physiological basis. Identify the approach that psychologist has employed to diagnose his patient. Also, enumerate the various factors that have been included in his approach.

Answers

1. (b)   2. (a)   3. (a)   4. (a)

CHAPTER 02

Therapeutic Approaches

In this Chapter...

- Introduction
- Nature and Process of Psychotherapy
- Types of Therapies
- Rehabilitation of the Mentally ILL

Introduction

There are various types of psychotherapy. Some of them focus on acquiring self-understanding, some other therapies are more action-oriented. The effectiveness of a therapeutic approach for a patient depends on a number of factors such as severity of the disorder, degree of distress faced by others and the availability of time, effort and money among others.

All therapeutic approaches are corrective and helping in nature. All these approaches involve interpersonal relationship between the patient and the therapist. These can be directive or non-directive in nature.

Nature and Process of Psychotherapy

Psychotherapy is a voluntary relationship between the **client** (patient) and the **therapist**. The purpose of the relationship is to help the client to solve the psychological problems being faced by her or him.

Psychotherapies aim at changing the abnormal behaviours, decreasing the sense of personal distress and helping the client to adapt better to her/his environment.

Characteristics of Psychotherapy

Psychotherapeutic approaches have the following characteristics

- There is a systematic application of principles underlying the different theories of therapy.
- Persons who have received practical training under expert supervision only can practice psychotherapy. An untrained person may unintentionally cause more harm than any good.
- The therapeutic situation involves a therapist and a client who seeks and receives help for her/his emotional problems.
- The interaction of these two persons i.e. the therapist and the client, results in the formation of the therapeutic relationship. This is a confidential, interpersonal and dynamic relationship. This human relationship is central to any type of psychological therapy and is the vehicle for change.

Goals of Psychotherapy

All psychotherapies aim at a few or all of the following goals

- Support client for attaining betterment
- Reduce emotional pressure

- Unfolding the potential for positive growth
- Modifying habits
- Changing thinking patterns
- Increasing self-awareness
- Improving interpersonal relations and communication
- Facilitating decision-making
- Becoming aware of one's choices in life
- Relating to one's social environment in a more creative and self-aware manner

Therapeutic Relationship

The special relationship between the client and the therapist is known as the therapeutic relationship or alliance. There are two major components of a therapeutic alliance, which are as follows

(i) The first component is the **contractual** (protected) nature of the relationship in which two willing individuals, the client and the therapist, enter into a **partnership** which aims at helping the client to overcome her/his problems.

(ii) The second component of therapeutic alliance is the limited duration of the therapy. This alliance lasts until the client becomes able to deal with her/his problems and take control of her/ his life.

This relationship has several unique properties. It is a trusting and confiding relationship. The high level of trust makes the client or patient to unburden himself to the therapist by saying all his psychological and personal problems. The therapist encourages this by being accepting, empathic, genuine and warm to the client.

The therapist conveys by her/his words and behaviours that she/he is not judging the client and will continue to show the same positive feelings towards the client even if the client is rude. This is the **unconditional positive regard** which the therapist has for his client.

Empathy Towards the Client

The therapist has empathy for the client. Empathy is different from sympathy. In sympathy, one has compassion and pity towards the suffering of another but is not able to feel like the other person. On the other hand, empathy is present when one is able to understand the plight of another person and feel like the other person.

It means understanding things from the other person's perspective. Empathy enriches the therapeutic relationship and transforms it into a healing relationship.

It is also important for the therapeutic alliance that the therapist must keep secret all the experiences and feelings shared by the patient to him.

The therapist must not exploit the trust and the confidence of the client in anyway. It is a professional relationship between the therapist and the client.

Parameters of Classification of Psychotherapies

The classification of psychotherapies is based on the following parameters

1. Cause of the Problem

Psychodynamic therapy views **intrapsychic conflicts** i.e. the conflicts that are present within the psyche of the person, are the source of psychological problems. According to behaviour therapies, psychological problems arise due to faulty learning of behaviours and cognitions. The existential therapies claims that the questions about the meaning of one's life and existence are the cause of psychological problems.

2. Existence of Cause

In the psychodynamic therapy, unfulfilled desires of childhood and unresolved childhood fears lead to intrapsychic conflicts. The behaviour therapy suggested that faulty conditioning patterns, faulty learning and faulty thinking and beliefs lead to abnormal (maladaptive) behaviours that, in turn, lead to psychological problems. It is the feeling of loneliness, alienation, sense of futility (insignificance) of one's existence, etc., which cause psychological problems.

3. Method of Treatment

Psychodynamic therapy uses the methods of free association and reporting of dreams to generate the **thoughts** and **feelings** of the client. This material is interpreted to the client to help her/him to confront and resolve the conflicts and thus overcome problems. Behaviour therapy identifies the faulty conditioning patterns and sets up alternate behavioural contingencies (events) to improve behaviour.

The cognitive methods employed in this type of theraphy challenge the faulty thinking patterns of the client and help her/him to overcome psychological distress.

The existential therapy provides a therapeutic environment which is positive, accepting and non-judgemental. The client is able to talk about the problems and the therapist acts as a facilitator. The client arrives at the solutions through a process of personal growth.

4. Nature of the Therapeutic Relationship between the Client and the Therapist

Psychodynamic therapy assumes that the therapist understands the intrapsychic conflicts of the client better than the client himself. The therapist interprets the thoughts and feelings of the client to her/him so that she/he gains an understanding of the same.

The behaviour therapy assumes that the therapist is able to detect the faulty behaviour and thought patterns of the client. The existential therapies emphasise that the therapist provides a **warm, empathic relationship** in which the client feels secure to explore the nature and causes of her/his problems by herself/himself.

5. Chief Benefit to the Client

Psychodynamic therapy values emotional insight as the important benefit that the client derives from the treatment. Emotional insight is present when the client understands her/his conflicts intellectually and able to accept the same emotionally and is able to change her/his emotions towards the conflicts. The client's symptoms and distresses reduces as a consequence of this emotional insight.

The behaviour therapy considers changing faulty behaviour and thought patterns to adaptive ones as the chief benefit of the treatment. Instituting adaptive or healthy behaviour and thought patterns ensures reduction of distress and removal of symptoms.

The humanistic therapy values **personal growth** as the main benefit. Personal growth is the process of increasing understanding of oneself and one's aspirations, emotions and motives.

6. Duration of the Treatment

The duration of classical psychoanalysis may continue for several years. Psychodynamic therapies are completed in 10–15 sessions. Behaviour and cognitive behaviour therapies as well as existential therapies are shorter and are completed in a few months.

Thus, different types of psychotherapies differ on multiple parameters. However, they all share the common method of providing treatment for psychological distress through psychological means.

Steps in the Formulation of a Client's Problem

Clinical formulation refers to formulating the problem of the client in the therapeutic model being used for the treatment. The clinical formulation has the following advantages

Understanding of the Problem The therapist is able to understand the full implications of the distress being experienced by the client.

Identification of the Areas to be Targeted for Treatment in Psychotherapy The theoretical formulation clearly identifies the problem areas to be targeted for therapy. Thus, if a client seeks help for inability to hold a job and reports inability to face superiors, the clinical formulation in behaviour therapy would state it as lack of assertiveness skills and anxiety. The target areas are identified as inability to assert oneself and heightened anxiety.

Choice of Techniques for Treatment The choice of techniques for treatment depends on the therapeutic system in which the therapist has been trained. However, even within this broad domain, the choice of techniques, timing of the techniques and expectations of outcome of the therapy depend upon the clinical formulation.

This clinical formulation is an ongoing process which may require reformulation as clinical insights are gained in the process of therapy.

Types of Therapies

Psychotherapies differ greatly in concepts, methods and techniques. They may be classified into three broad groups, *viz* the **psychodynamic, behaviour** and **existential psychotherapies**. Psychodynamic therapy emerged first followed by behaviour therapy, while the existential therapies which are also called the **third force**, emerged last. Behaviour therapy, cognitive therapy, humanistic-existential therapy and alternative therapies are discussed as follows

Behaviour Therapy

This therapy claims that psychological distress arises because of faulty behaviour patterns or thought patterns. It is focused on the behaviour and thoughts of the client in the present. The past is relevant only to the extent of understanding the origins of the faulty behaviour and thought patterns.

Behaviour therapy consists of a large set of specific techniques and interventions. The symptoms of the client and the clinical diagnosis are the guiding factors in the selection of the specific techniques or interventions to be applied in the behaviour therapy.

Treatment of phobias or excessive and crippling fears would require the use of one set of techniques, while that of anger outbursts would require another. A depressed client would be treated differently from a client who is anxious.

Method of Treatment

Behavioural analysis is conducted to find malfunctioning behaviours, the antecedents of faulty learning and the factors that maintain or continue faulty learning.

Malfunctioning behaviours are those behaviours which cause distress to the client. **Antecedent factors** are those factors which affect the person to indulge in that behaviour. **Maintaining factors** are those factors which lead to the persistence of the faulty behaviour.

The aim of the treatment is to eliminate the faulty behaviours and substitute them with adaptive behaviour patterns. The therapist does this through establishing antecedent operations and consequent operations.

Antecedent operations control behaviour by changing something that precedes such a behaviour. The change can be done by increasing or decreasing the reinforcing value of a particular consequence which is called **establishing operation**. For example, if a child creates trouble in eating dinner, then decrease the quantity of food served at tea time.

It will increase the hunger at dinner and he will take proper quantity of food at dinner. Praise the child for this behaviour. Here, the antecedent operation is the reduction of food at tea time and the consequent operation is praising the child for eating dinner properly.

Behavioural Techniques

There are various techniques for changing behaviour. The principles of these techniques are to reduce the arousal level of the client, alter behaviour through **classical conditioning**[1] or with different contingencies of reinforcements, as well as to use **vicarious** (indirect) learning procedures.

Some techniques of behaviour modification are as follows

Negative Reinforcement

Negative reinforcement is a major technique of behaviour modification. Responses that lead organisms to get rid of painful stimuli or avoid and escape from them provide negative reinforcement.

For example, one learns to put on woollen clothes, burn firewood or use electric heaters to avoid the unpleasant cold weather. Person learns to move away from dangerous stimuli because they provide negative reinforcement.

Positive Reinforcement

If an adaptive behaviour occurs rarely, positive reinforcement is given to increase the deficit. For example, if a child does not do homework regularly, positive reinforcement may be used by the child's mother by preparing the child's favourite dish whenever she/he does homework at the appointed time. The positive reinforcement of food will increase the behaviour of doing homework at the appointed time.

Aversive Conditioning

It refers to repeated association of undesired response with an adverse consequence. For example, an alcoholic is given a mild electric shock and asked to smell the alcohol.

With repeated pairings, the smell of alcohol is aversive as the pain of the shock is associated with it and the person will give up alcohol.

Token Economy

Person with behavioural problems can be given a token as a reward every time when a wanted behaviour occurs. The tokens are collected and exchanged for a reward such as an outing for the patient or a treat for the child. This is known as token economy.

Differential Reinforcement

Unwanted behaviour can be reduced and wanted behaviour can be increased simultaneously through differential reinforcement. **Positive reinforcement** for the wanted behaviour and **negative reinforcement** for the unwanted behaviour attempted together may be one such method. The other method is to positively reinforce the wanted behaviour and ignore the unwanted behaviour. The latter method is less painful and equally effective.

For example, a girl cries and refuses to talk (sulk) when she is not taken to the cinema. The parent is instructed to take her to the cinema if she does not cry and sulk. The parent is also instructed to ignore the girl when she cries and sulks. Gradually, the wanted behaviour of politely asking to be taken to the cinema increases and the unwanted behaviour of crying and sulking decreases.

Systematic Desensitisation

Systematic desensitisation is a technique introduced by **Wolpe** for treating phobias or irrational fears. The client is interviewed to generate fear-provoking situations. The therapist relaxes the client and asks the client to think about the least anxiety-provoking situation.

The client is asked to stop thinking of the fearful situation if the slightest tension is felt. After some sessions, the client is able to imagine more severe fear-provoking situations while maintaining the relaxation. The client gets systematically desensitised (stop being sensitive) to the fear.

---

1 Classical Conditioning It is a type of learning that happens unconsciously.

Principle of Reciprocal (Mutual) Inhibition

This principle states that the presence of two mutually opposing forces at the same time, inhibits the weaker force. Thus, the relaxation response is first built up and mildly anxiety-provoking scene is imagined, through which the anxiety is overcome by the relaxation. The client is able to tolerate progressively greater levels of anxiety because of her/his relaxed state.

Modelling

Modelling is the procedure wherein the client learns to behave in a certain way by observing the behaviour of a role model or the therapist who initially acts as the role model. **Vicarious learning** i.e. learning by observing others, is used and through a process of rewarding small changes in the behaviour, the client gradually learns to acquire the behaviour of the model.

The skill of the therapist lies in conducting an accurate behavioural analysis and building a treatment package with the appropriate techniques.

Relaxation Procedures

Relaxation procedures are used to decrease the anxiety levels. For instance, progressive muscular relaxation and meditation induce a state of relaxation. In progressive muscular relaxation, the client is taught to contract individual muscle groups in order to give the awareness of tenseness or muscular tension. After the client has learnt to tense the muscle group such as the forearm, the client is asked to let go the tension. With repeated practice the client learns to relax all the muscles of the body.

Cognitive Therapy

These therapies revealed the cause of psychological distress in irrational thoughts and beliefs.

Following approaches have been used as cognitive therapy

Rational Emotive Therapy (RET)

It was formulated by **Albert Ellis**. The central idea of this therapy is that irrational beliefs mediate between the **antecedent events**[2] and their consequences. The first step in RET is the Antecedent Belief-Consequence (ABC) analysis. Antecedent events, which caused the psychological distress, are noted.

The client is also interviewed to find the irrational beliefs, which are distorting the present reality. These beliefs are characterised by thoughts with 'musts' and 'shoulds', i.e. things 'must' and 'should' be in a particular manner.

The distorted perception of the antecedent event due to the irrational belief leads to the consequence i.e. negative emotions and behaviours. Irrational beliefs are assessed through questionnaires and interviews.

In the process of RET, the irrational beliefs are opposed by the therapist through a process of **non-directive questioning**. The questions make the client to think deeper into her/his assumptions about life and problems. Gradually, the client is able to change the irrational beliefs by making a change in her/his philosophy about life. The rational belief system replaces the irrational belief system and there is a reduction in psychological distress.

Aaron Beck's Cognitive Therapy

Aaron Beck gave another cognitive therapy. His theory of psychological distress is characterised by anxiety or depression. It states that childhood experiences provided by the family and society develop core schemas or systems, which include beliefs and action patterns in the individual.

Negative thoughts which develop are persistent irrational thoughts. These are characterised by cognitive distortions. For example, 'Nobody loves me', 'I am ugly', 'I am stupid', etc.

Cognitive distortions (deformation) are ways of thinking which are general in nature but distort the reality in a negative manner. These patterns of thought are called **dysfunctional cognitive structures**.

Repeated occurrence of these thoughts leads to the development of feelings of **anxiety** and **depression**. The aim of the therapy is to achieve cognitive restructuring which, in turn, reduces anxiety and depression. The therapist uses questioning, which is gentle, non-threatening disputation of the client's beliefs and thoughts. Examples of such questions are as follows

- Why should everyone love you?
- What does it mean to you to succeed?

The questions make the client think in a direction opposite to that of the negative automatic thoughts whereby she/he gains insight into the nature of her/his dysfunctional schemas and is able to alter her/his cognitive restructuring which, in turn, reduces, anxiety and depression.

Cognitive Behaviour Therapy (CBT)

Cognitive behaviour therapy is the most popular therapy. It is a short and efficacious treatment for a wide range of psychological disorders such as anxiety, depression, panic attacks and borderline personality disorder, etc.

---

2 Antecedent Events The events, actions or circumstances that occur immediately before a behaviour.

It adopts a biopsychosocial approach to the delineation (explain in detail) of psychopathology. It combines cognitive therapy with behavioural techniques. It addresses the biological aspects through relaxation procedures. The psychologist through behaviour and cognitive therapy techniques and the social ones with environmental manipulations makes CBT a comprehensive technique which is easy to use and is applicable to a variety of disorders.

Humanistic-Existential Therapy

This therapy claims that psychological distress arises from feelings of loneliness, alienation and an inability to find meaning and genuine fulfilment in life. Human beings are motivated by the desire for personal growth and self-actualisation and an innate need to grow emotionally. When these needs are controlled by society and family, human beings experience psychological distress.

Self-actualisation is defined as an inborn force that moves the person to become more complex, balanced and integrated. As lack of food and water causes distress, frustration of self-actualisation also causes distress.

Healing occurs when the client is able to perceive the obstacles to self-actualisation in her/his life and is able to remove them.

The therapy creates a permissive, non-judgemental and accepting atmosphere in which the client's emotions can be freely expressed and the complexity, balance and integration could be achieved. The fundamental assumption is that the client has the freedom and responsibility to control her/his own behaviour.

The therapist is a facilitator and guide and the client himself is responsible for the success of therapy.

The main aim of the therapy is to expand the client's awareness. Healing takes place by a process of understanding the unique personal experience of the client by herself/himself. The client initiates the process of self-growth through which healing takes place.

Existential Therapy

Victor Frankl, a psychiatrist and neurologist propounded the **Logotherapy.** Logos is the Greek word for soul and logotherapy means treatment for the soul. Frankl calls this process of finding meaning even in life-threatening circumstances as the process of meaning making.

The basis of meaning making is a person's quest for finding the spiritual truth of one's existence. The spiritual unconscious include love, aesthetic awareness and values of life.

Neurotic anxieties arise when the problems of life are attached to the physical, psychological or spiritual aspects of one's existence. Frankl emphasised the role of spiritual anxieties in leading to meaninglessness. Hence, it may be called an existential anxiety i.e. neurotic anxiety of spiritual origin.

The goal of logotherapy is to help the patients to find meaning and responsibility in their life irrespective of their life circumstances. The therapist emphasises the unique nature of the patient's life and encourages them to find meaning in their life.

Client-centred Therapy

Client-centred therapy was given by **Carl Rogers**. Rogers combined scientific determination with the individualised practice of client-centred psychotherapy. Rogers brought into psychotherapy the concept of self, with freedom and choice as the core of one's being.

The therapy provides a warm relationship in which the client can reconnect with her/his disintegrated feelings. The therapist shows empathy, i.e. understanding the client's experience. Empathy sets up an emotional resonance between the therapist and the client.

Unconditional positive regard indicates that the positive warmth of the therapist is not dependent on what the client reveals or does in the therapy sessions. This unique unconditional warmth ensures that the client feels secure, can trust the therapist. The client feels secure enough to explore her/his feelings.

The therapist reflects the feelings of the client in a non-judgemental manner. The reflection is achieved by rephrasing the statements of the client i.e. seeking simple clarifications to enhance the meaning of the client's statements.

This process of reflection helps the client to become integrated. Personal relationships improve with an increase in adjustment. This therapy helps a client to become her/his real self with the therapist working as a facilitator.

Gestalt Therapy

The German word Gestalt means **whole**. This therapy was given by Freiderick (Fritz) Perls together with his wife Laura Perls. The goal of this therapy is to increase an individual's self-awareness and self-acceptance. The client is taught to recognise the bodily processes and the emotions that are being blocked out from awareness. The therapist does this by encouraging the client to act out fantasies about feelings and conflicts. This therapy can also be used in group settings.

Factors Contributing to Healing in Psychotherapy

There are several factors which contribute to the healing process. Some of these factors are as follows

- A major factor in the healing is the techniques adopted by the therapist and the implementation of the same with the patient/client. If the behavioural system and the CBT school are adopted to heal an anxious client, the relaxation procedures and the cognitive restructuring largely contribute to the healing.

- The therapeutic alliance, which is formed between the therapist and the patient/client, has healing properties, because of the regular availability of the therapist and the warmth and empathy provided by the therapist.

- At the beginning of therapy, while the patient/client is being interviewed in the initial sessions to understand the nature of the problem, she/he unburdens the emotional problems being faced. This process of emotional unburdening is known as **catharsis** and it has healing properties.

- There are several non-specific factors associated with psychotherapy. Some of these factors are attributed to the patient/client and some to the therapist. These factors are called **non-specific** because they occur across different systems of psychotherapy and across different clients/patients and different therapists.

- Non-specific factors attributable (available) to the client/patient are motivation for change, expectation of improvement due to the treatment, etc. These are called **patient variables**. Non-specific factors attributable to the therapist are positive nature, absence of unresolved emotional conflicts, presence of good mental health, etc. These are called **therapist variables**.

Ethics in Psychotherapy

Some of the ethical standards that need to be practised by professional psychotherapists are

- Consent of client should be taken.
- Confidentiality of the client should be maintained.
- Alleviating personal distress and suffering should be the goal of all attempts of the therapist.
- Integrity of the practitioner-client relationship is important.
- Respect for human rights and dignity.
- Professional competence and skills are essential.

Alternative Therapies

There are alternative treatment possibilities to the conventional drug treatment or psychotherapy. There are many alternative therapies such as yoga, meditation, acupuncture, herbal remedies and so on.

Yoga and Meditation

In the past 25 years, yoga and meditation have gained popularity as treatment programmes for psychological distress. Yoga is an ancient Indian technique detailed in the *Ashtanga Yoga* of Patanjali's *Yoga Sutras*. Yoga is commonly refer to the *asanas* or body posture component or to breathing practices or *pranayama*.

Yoga techniques enhance well-being, mood, attention, mental focus and stress tolerance. Proper training by a skilled teacher and a 30-minute practice every day will maximise the benefits. Insomnia is treated with yoga. Yoga also reduces the time to go to sleep and improves the quality of sleep.

Meditation refers to the practice of focusing attention on breath or on an object or thought or a *mantra*. In *Vipasana* meditation, also known as **mindfulness-based meditation**, there is no fixed object or thought to hold the attention. The person passively observes the various bodily sensations and thoughts that are passing through in her or his awareness. Prevention of repeated episodes of depression may be treated by mindfulness-based meditation or *Vipasana*.

Sudarshana Kriya Yoga

In Sudarshana Kriya Yoga (SKY) the rapid breathing techniques are used to induce hyperventilation. It is beneficial for the treatment of stress, anxiety, Post-Traumatic Stress Disorder (PTSD), depression, stress related medical illnesses, substance abuse and rehabilitation of criminal offenders. Research conducted at the National Institute of Mental Health and Neurosciences (NIMHANS), India has shown that SKY reduces depression. Further, alcoholic patients who practice SKY have reduced depression and stress levels.

Kundalini Yoga

Kundalini Yoga is taught in the USA. It is effective in the treatment of mental disorders. The Institute for Non-linear Science, University of California, San Diego, USA has found that Kundalini Yoga is effective in the treatment of obsessive compulsive disorder. *Kundalini Yoga* combines *pranayama* or breathing techniques with chanting of *mantras*.

Rehabilitation of the Mentally Ill

The treatment of psychological disorders has two components i.e. reduction of symptoms and improving the level of functioning or quality of life. In the case of milder (lighter) disorders such as generalised anxiety disorder, reactive depression or phobia, reduction of symptoms, etc., is associated with an improvement in the quality of life.

However, in the case of severe mental disorders such as schizophrenia, reduction of symptoms may not be associated with an improvement in the quality of life.

Rehabilitation is required to help patients become self-sufficient. The aim of rehabilitation is to empower the patient to become a productive member of society to the extent possible. In rehabilitation, the patients are given occupational therapy, social skills training and vocational therapy. These are discussed as follows

- In occupational therapy, the patients are taught skills such as candle making, paper bag making and weaving to help them to form a work discipline.
- Social skills training helps the patients to develop interpersonal skills through role play, imitation and instruction. The objective is to teach the patient to function in a social group.
- Cognitive retraining is given to improve the basic cognitive functions of attention, memory and executive functions. After the patient improves sufficiently, vocational training is given wherein the patient is helped to gain skills necessary to undertake productive employment.

Chapter Practice

Objective Questions

• Multiple Choice Questions

1. Salim does not like to play in the park as he is allergic to dust. Hence, dust is______ .

(a) Aversive conditioning
(b) Positive reinforcement
(c) Differential reinforcement
(d) Negative reinforcement

Ans. (d) Dust is a negative reinforcement which is a major technique of behaviour modification.

2. Which of the following involves associating of undesired response with an adverse consequence?

(a) Aversive conditioning   (b) Token economy
(c) Modelling   (d) Positive reinforcement

Ans. (a) Aversive conditioning involves associating of undesired response with an adverse consequence.

3. Which of the following is/are the behavioural technique?

1. Negative Reinforcement
2. Aversive Conditioning
3. Token Economy
4. Transference

Choose the correct option

(a) 1,2,3   (b) 2,3,4   (c) 3,4,1   (d) 1,2,4

Ans. (a) Negative reinforcement, aversive conditioning and token economy are behavioural techniques while transference is a modality of treatment.

4. In _________therapy a person is given a token as reward for behaving in a required way.

(a) Reciprocal inhibition
(b) Vicarious learning
(c) Systematic desensitisation
(d) Token economy

Ans (d) In Token economy therapy a person is given a token as reward for behaving in a required way.

5. Systematic desensitisation is used to treat _________.

(a) Schizophrenia   (b) ADHD
(c) Phobias   (d) Autism

Ans. (c) Systematic desensitisation is used to treat phobias or irrational fears.

6. Naina was shown by her elder sister how to behave in front of the guest. This technique of learning is known as _________.

(a) Token economy   (b) Modelling
(c) Rational emotive therapy (d) Relaxation therapy

Ans. (b) The technique of learning shown by Nainas elder sister i.e. how to behave in front of the guest is known as modelling. Modelling is the procedure wherein the client learns to behave in a certain way by observing the behaviour of a role model.

8. Who propounded the logotherapy?

(a) Sigmund Freud   (b) Victor Frankl
(c) Ivan Pavlov   (d) B.F. Skinner

Ans. (b) Victor Frankl, a psychiatrist and neurologist propounded the logotherapy.

7. Learning by observing others is known as

(a) Reciprocal inhibition
(b) Vicarious learning
(c) Systematic desensitisation
(d) Token economy

Ans (b) Learning by observing others is known as Vicarious learning.

9. Which of the following is true about Gestalt therapy?

1. Gestalt is a German word which means whole.
2. This therapy was given by Freiderick (Fritz) Perls together with his wife Laura Perls.
3. The goal of this therapy is to increase an individual's self-awareness and self-acceptance.
4. This therapy cannot be used in group settings.

Choose the correct option

(a) 1,2,3   (b) 2,3, 4
(c) 1,3,4   (d) 2,4, 1

Ans (a) The German word Gestalt means whole. This therapy was given by Freiderick (Fritz) Perls together with his wife Laura Perls. The goal of this therapy is to increase an individual's self-awareness and self-acceptance.

10. Which of the following statements are correct about the client-centred therapy?
1. It was given by Carl Rogers.
2. It combined scientific determination with the individualised practice of client-centred psychotherapy.
3. The therapist must show no empathy.
4. It provides a warm relationship in which the client can reconnect with her/his disintegrated feelings.

Choose the correct option
(a) 1,3,4   (b) 1,2,4   (c) 1,2,3   (d) 3,2,1

Ans. (b) The client-centred therapy was given by Carl Rogers. Here, scientific determination is combined with individualised practice of therapy. The client is provided such an environment where the client can reconnect with his/her disintegrated feelings.

11. Raman has been diagnosed with a psychological disorder. He approached a psychologist who prescribed certain psychotherapies for him, The goal of psychotherapies is to
(a) change the maladaptive behaviours
(b) decrease the sense of personal distress
(c) help the client to adapt better to his environment
(d) All of the above

Ans. (d) The goal of psychotherapies is to change the maladaptive behaviours, decrease the sense of personal distress, help the client to adapt better to his environment.

12. Which of the following is not an alternative therapy?
(a) Yoga   (b) Meditation
(c) Drugs   (d) Acupuncture

Ans. (c) Drugs, is not an alternative therapy. Yoga, Acupuncture, meditation and herbal therapies are alternative therapies.

13. In ______________, the rapid breathing techniques are used to induce hyperventilation.
(a) Kundalini yoga   (b) Vipasana
(c) Sudarshana Kriya Yoga   (d) Ashtanga

Ans. (c) In Sudarshana Kriya Yoga (SKY), the rapid breathing techniques are used to induce hyperventilation. It is beneficial for the treatment of stress, anxiety, Post-Traumatic Stress Disorder (PTSD), depression, etc.

14. Sanjay becomes silent during the therapy session, recalls trivial details without recalling the emotional ones, misses appointments and comes late for therapy sessions. Sanjay is in __________.
(a) Shock   (b) Denial
(c) Unconscious resistance   (d) Attitude

Ans. (c) Sanjay is in unconscious resistance in this process Unconscious resistance is assured to be present when the client becomes silent during the therapy session, recalls trivial details without recalling the emotional ones, misses appointments and comes late for therapy sessions.

15. Sagar was taught skills such as candle making, paper bag making and weaving to help him to form a work discipline. This is known as __________.
(a) Positive reinforcement   (b) Occupational therapy
(c) Alternative therapy   (d) Behavioural therapy

Ans. (b) To induce work discipline, Sagar was taught skills such as candle making, paper bag making and weaving. The given therapy is known as occupational therapy.

• Assertion-Reasoning MCQs

Directions (Q. Nos. 1-4) *Each of these questions contains two statements, Assertion (A) and Reason (R). Each of these questions also has four alternative choices, any one of which is the correct answer. You have to select one of the codes (a), (b), (c) and (d) given below.*
(a) Both A and R are true and R is the correct explanation of A
(b) Both A and R are true, but R is not the correct explanation of A
(c) A is true, but R is false
(d) A is false, but R is true

1. **Assertion** (A) In systematic desensitisation client asked to think about the least anxiety-provoking situations.

Reason (R) The client hence, learns to deal with fearful situations.

Ans. (a) In systematic desensitisation client learns to deal with fearful situation as he is interviewed to deal with fear provoking situation and then asked to think about least anxiety provoking situation. Thus, Both A and R are true and R is not the correct explanation of A.

2. **Assertion** (A) In principle of reciprocal inhibition, the relaxation response is first built up and a mildly anxiety-provoking scene is imagined, through which the anxiety is overcome by the relaxation.

Reason (R) The presence of two mutually opposing forces at the same time, inhibits the weaker force.

Ans. (a) The principle of reciprocal inhibition states that the presence of two mutually opposing forces at the same time, inhibits the weaker force. Thus, the relaxation response is first built up and a mildly anxiety-provoking scene is imagined, through which the anxiety is overcome by the relaxation. Hence, Both A and R are true and R is the correct explanation of A.

3. Assertion (A) Rational Emotive Therapy was formulated by Albert Ellis.

Reason (R) The first step in RET is the Antecedent Belief-Consequence analysis.

Ans. (b) Both A and R are true but R is not the correct explanation of A. Rational Emotive Therapy was formulated by Albert Ellis. Antecedent Belief-Consequence analysis is the first step in RET.

4. Assertion (A) Cognitive distortions are ways of thinking that may be the cause behind depression.

Reason (R) Repeated occurrence of negative thoughts leads to the development of feelings of anxiety and depression.

Ans. (a) Cognitive distortions are ways of thinking which are general in nature but which distort the reality in a negative manner. Repeated occurrence of these thoughts leads to the development of feelings of anxiety and depression. Hence, Both A and R are true and R is the correct explanation of A.

• Case Based MCQs

1. Manish is a hard-core alcoholic. He had started drinking in his school days and has been drinking alcohol since the age of seventeen. Now he is 32 and highly motivated to give up his habit. However, no matter how hard he tries after a period of abstinence comes a phase of relapse.

Around two years back he joined an alcohol support group. From there he got motivated to attend a few psychotherapy sessions. He found these sessions quite relevant. Recently, his psychologists started a new technique. In this technique, Manish is given a slight electric shock whenever he drinks alcohol. He has responded positively to this approach and after years his alcohol consumption has come down remarkably.

His family was initially apprehensive about this approach but after looking at the positive results they are now in support of the therapy.

(i) What is this new therapy that Manish is being given by his psychologists called?
 (a) Aversive conditioning (b) Token economy
 (c) Positive reinforcement (d) Systematic desensitisation

Ans. (a) The new therapy that Manish is being given by his psychologists is called Aversive conditioning. It refers to repeated association of undesired response with an adverse consequence.

(ii) How this therapy helping Manish to get rid of alcoholism?

 (a) Electric shock makes Manish unable to drink.
 (b) Electric shock hinders with the taste of the alcohol.
 (c) The association of electric shock with alcohol intake makes alcohol intake less attractive.
 (d) Electric shock gives bad side effects with alcohol.

Ans. (c) This therapy helped Manish to get rid of alcoholism as association of electric shock with alcohol intake makes alcohol intake less attractive.

(iii) Which type of learning is seen in the given psychotherapy?
 (a) Classical conditioning (b) Operant conditioning
 (c) Random learning (d) None

Ans. (a) Classical conditioning is seen in the given psychotherapy. Any learning which is taught by conditioning a required response to a stimulus is known as classical conditioning.

(iv) Which of the following types of psychotherapy is aversive conditioning?
 (a) Biomedical technique
 (b) Alternative technique
 (c) Behavioural technique
 (d) Cognitive therapy

Ans. (c) Behavioural technique is a type of psychotherapy which is aversive conditioning.

(v) In this new therapy, what aversive response is being subjected to Manish for drinking?
 (a) A medicine
 (b) A high degree electric shock
 (c) A mild degree electric shock
 (d) Imprisonment

Ans. (c) Manish is being given a mild degree of electric shock whenever he drinks. This is to condition him to dislike drinking as he would eventually associate drinking with the pain of electric shock.

(vi) **Assertion** (A) In aversive therapy a token is given every time a person behaves in a required manner.

Reason (R) The client leaves the bad habit due to repeated pairing of bad behaviour and aversive response.

 (a) Both A and R are true and R is the correct explanation of A
 (b) Both A and R are true, but R is not the correct explanation of A
 (c) A is true, but R is false
 (d) A is false, but R is true

Ans. (d) In aversive conditioning, repeated association of undesired response is done with an adverse consequence. The client associates and leaves the bad habit due to repeated pairing of bad behaviour and aversive response. Thus, A is false, but R is true.

Subjective Questions

• Short Answer (SA) Type Questions

1. What do we mean by psychotherapy? Explain.

Ans. Psychotherapy is a voluntary relationship between the client (patient) and the therapist. The purpose of the relationship is to help the client to solve the psychological problems being faced by her or him.

Psychotherapies aim at changing the maladaptive behaviours, decreasing the sense of personal distress and helping the client to adapt better to her/his environment. Inadequate marital, occupational and social adjustment also require that major changes be made in an individual's personal environment.

2. State four characteristics of psychotherapeutic approaches. **(All India 2015)**

Ans. Psychotherapeutic approaches have the following characteristics

(i) There is systematic application of principles underlying the different theories of therapy

(ii) Persons who have received practical training under expert supervision only he can practice psychotherapy. An untrained person may unintentionally cause more harm than any good.

(iii) The therapeutic situation involves a therapist and a client who seeks and receives help for her/his emotional problems.

(iv) The interaction of these two persons i.e. the therapist and the client results in the formation of the therapeutic relationship. This is a confidential, interpersonal and dynamic relationship. This human relationship is central to any sort of psychological therapy and is the vehicle for change.

3. What are the major components of a therapeutic alliance?

Ans. There are two major components of a therapeutic alliance are as follows

(i) The first component is the contractual nature of the relationship in which two willing individuals, the client and the therapist, enter into a partnership which aims at helping the client to overcome her/his problems.

(ii) The second component of therapeutic alliance is the limited duration of the therapy. This alliance lasts until the client becomes able to deal with her/his problems and take control of her/his life.

4. Explain the main feature of therapeutic relationship.

Ans. Therapeutic relationship has several unique features which are as follows

(i) It is a trusting and confiding relationship.

(ii) The high level of trust enables the client to unburden herself/himself to the therapist and confide her/his psychological and personal problems to the latter.

(iii) The therapist encourages this by being accepting, empathic, genuine and warm to the client.

(iv) The therapist conveys by her/his words and behaviours that she/he is not judging the client and will continue to show the same positive feelings towards the client even if the client is rude.

(v) The therapeutic alliance also requires that the therapist must keep strict confidentiality of the experiences, events, feelings or thoughts disclosed by the client.

(vi) The therapist must not exploit the trust and the confidence of the client in anyway.

(vii) It is a professional relationship between the therapist and the client.

5. Explain positive regards for others in the context of counselling.

Ans. Unconditional positive regard indicates that the positive warmth of the therapist is not dependent on what the client reveals or does in the therapy sessions. This unique unconditional warmth ensures that the client feels secure, can trust the therapist and feels secure enough to explore her/his feelings. The therapist reflects the feelings of the client in a non-judgemental manner.

The reflection is achieved by rephrasing the statements of the client i.e. seeking simple clarifications to enhance the meaning of the client's statements. This process of reflection helps the client to become integrated. This therapy helps a client to become her/his real self with the therapist working as a facilitator.

6. Nikhil has some psychological disorders. He is taking psychoanalytic therapy. What are the different stages and duration of his treatment?

Ans. Psychoanalytic therapy of Nikhil consists of three stages. In **stage one** he becomes familiar with the routines, establishes a therapeutic relationship with the analyst. He gets some relief with the process of recollecting the superficial materials from the consciousness about the past and present troublesome events.

Stage two is the middle phase, which is a long process and it is characterised by transference, resistance on the part of Nikhil and confrontation and clarification, i.e. working through on the therapist's part. All these processes finally lead to insight.

Stage three is the termination phase where in the relationship with the analyst and Nikhil is dissolved and he prepares to leave the therapy.

7. Explain psychological distress according to the behaviour therapy. Describe any one behavioural technique. **(All India 2017)**

Ans. According to the behaviour therapies, psychological distress arises because of faulty behaviour patterns or thought patterns. It is focused on the behaviour and thoughts of the client in the present.

The past is relevant only to the extent of understanding the origins of the faulty behaviour and thought patterns. Only the faulty patterns are corrected in the present. Behaviour therapy consists of a large set of specific techniques and interventions. The symptoms of the client and the clinical diagnosis are the guiding factors in the selection of the specific techniques of behaviour therapy. One behavioural technique is given below

Aversive Conditioning is a major technique of behaviour modification. Aversive conditioning refers to repeated association of undesired response with an aversive consequence. For example, an alcoholic is given a mild electric shock and asked to smell the alcohol. With repeated pairings the smell of alcohol is aversive as the pain of the shock is associated with it and the person will give up alcohol.

8. What is behaviour therapy? How is behaviour therapy used to treat phobia?

Ans. Behaviour therapy is a term that describes a broad range of techniques which are used to change maladaptive behaviour. It is focussed on the behaviour and thoughts of the client in present. It is a technique introduced by Wolpe for treating phobias or irrational fears. The client is interviewed to elicit fear-provoking situations.

The therapist relaxes the client and asks the client to think about the least anxiety- provoking situation. The client is asked to stop thinking of the fearful situation if the slightest tension is felt. After some sessions, the client is able to imagine more severe fear-provoking situations while maintaining the relaxation. The client gets systematically desensitised to the fear.

9. Explain negative reinforcement and positive reinforcement for behaviour modification.

Ans. **Negative Reinforcement** It is a major technique of behaviour modification. Responses that lead organisms to get rid of painful stimuli or avoid and escape from them provide negative reinforcement.

For example, one learns to put on woolen clothes, burn firewood or use electric heaters to avoid the unpleasant cold weather. Person learns to move away from dangerous stimuli because they provide negative reinforcement.

Positive Reinforcement If an adaptive behaviour occurs rarely, positive reinforcement is given to increase the deficit. For example, if a child does not do homework regularly, positive reinforcement may be used by the child's mother by preparing the child's favourite dish whenever she/he does homework at the appointed time. The positive reinforcement of food will increase the behaviour of doing homework at the appointed time.

10. Ankit rarely does his homework regularly. Her mother promised him to prepare his favourite dish whenever he does homework at the appointed time. Identify the reinforcement given by Ankit's mother? How does it benefit the person?

Ans. In the given case, Ankit's mother is giving positive reinforcement. Positive reinforcement is a process that strengthens the likelihood of a particular response of adding a stimulus after the positive reinforcement is used by the child's mother by preparing the child's favourite dish whenever he does homework at the appointed time. The positive reinforcement of food will increase the behaviour of doing homework at the appointed time. Persons with behavioural problems can be given a token as a reward every time a wanted behaviour occurs. Thus, a positive reinforcement is given to increase the deficit.

11. What kind of problems is cognitive behaviour therapy best suited for?

Ans. Cognitive behaviour therapy is a short and efficacious treatment for a wide range of psychological disorders such as anxiety, depression, panic attacks and borderline personality, etc. It is the most popular therapy. It adopts a biopsychosocial approach to the delineation of psychopathology. It combines cognitive therapy with behavioural techniques. It addresses the biological aspects through relaxation procedures.

The psychologist through behaviour and cognitive therapy techniques and the sociologist with environmental manipulations makes CBT a comprehensive technique which is easy to use and is applicable to a variety of disorders.

12. What is the meaning of logotherapy? **(Delhi 2016)**

Ans. Victor Frankl, a psychiatrist and neurologist propounded the logotherapy. Logos is the Greek word for soul and logotherapy means treatment for the soul. Frankl calls this process of finding meaning even in life-threatening circumstances as the process of meaning making. The basis of meaning making is a person's quest for finding the spiritual truth of one's existence.

The spiritual unconscious includes love, aesthetic awareness, and values of life. Neurotic anxieties arise when the problems of life are attached to the physical, psychological or spiritual aspects of one's existence.

The goal of logotherapy is to help the patients to find meaning and responsibility in their life irrespective of their life circumstances. The therapist emphasises the unique nature of the patient's life and encourages them to find meaning in their life.

13. Discuss briefly Gestalt Therapy. **(Delhi 2015)**

Or Discuss Client-centred Therapy.

Ans. Gestalt Therapy was given by Freiderick (Fritz) Perls together with his wife Laura Perls. The goal of Gestalt therapy is to increase an individual's self-awareness and self-acceptance. The client is taught to recognise the bodily processes and the emotions that are being blocked out from awareness. The therapist does this by encouraging the client to act out fantasies about feelings and conflicts. This therapy can also be used in group settings.

Client-centred Therapy Client-centred therapy was given by **Carl Rogers**. The therapy provides a warm relationship in which the client can reconnect with her/his disintegrated feelings. The therapist shows empathy, i.e. understanding the client's experience. Empathy sets up an emotional resonance between the therapist and the client.

14. The aim of the behaviour therapy is to extinguish the faulty behaviour. Illustrate with example how antecedent operations and consequent operations are used in this therapy.

Ans. The aim of the behaviour therapy is to extinguish the faulty behaviour and substitute them with adaptive behaviour pattern.

The therapist does this through establishing antecedent operations and consequent operations. Antecedent operations control behaviour by changing something that precedes such a behaviour. The change can be done by increasing or decreasing the reinforcing value of a particular consequence. This is called establishing operation.

For example, if a child gives trouble in eating dinner, an establishing operation would be, to decrease the quantity of food served at tea time. This would increase the hunger at dinner and thereby increase the reinforcing value of food at dinner. Praising the child when she/he eats properly tends to encourage this behaviour. It establishes the response of eating dinner.

15. How would a social learning theorist account for a phobic fear of lizards/cockroaches? How would a psychoanalyst account for the same phobia?**(NCERT)**

Or A person has a phobia of cockroaches. Explain this phobia from the social learning perspective and psychoanalyst view point by giving examples.
(CBSE 2018)

Ans. Social learning theories work on the principle that our experience be it positive or negative such as phobia of lizards/cockroaches are the result of learning process which start early in life. Small children can play with snakes, they are not aware of danger involved. For them, it is just another play object, as they grow up the fear of these things are instilled by their parents and society which is reinforced and accounts for reaction like phobia.

A psychoanalytical account for the same phobia could involve attribution to unconscious and repressed experiences. For example, suppose in your childhood you watched a group of roudy boys brutally torturing a cockroach/snake which eventually died, although you going about the incidence after some days but it might remain in back of your mind forever and disturb you emotionally.

16. What are the Alternative Therapies for the conventional drug treatment or psychotherapy. Mention Yoga and Meditation as Alternative Therapies.

Ans. There are alternative treatment possibilities to the conventional drug treatment or psychotherapy. There are many alternative therapies such as yoga, meditation, accupuncture, herbal remedies and so on.

Yoga and Meditation is an ancient Indian technique detailed in the *Ashtanga Yoga* of Patanjali's *Yoga Sutras*. Yoga is commonly refer to the *asanas* or body posture component or to breathing practices or *pranayama*.

Yoga techniques enhance well-being, mood, attention, mental focus and stress tolerance. Proper training by a skilled teacher and a 30-minute practice every day will maximise the benefits. Insomnia is treated with yoga. Yoga also reduces the time to go to sleep and improves the quality of sleep.

Meditation refers to the practice of focusing attention on breath or on an object or thought or a *mantra*. In *Vipasana* meditation, also known as mindfulness-based meditation, there is no fixed object or thought to hold the attention.

• Long Answer (LA) Type Questions

1. Describe the nature and scope of psychotherapy. Highlight the importance of therapeutic relationship in psychotherapy. **(NCERT)**

Or Explain the importance of therapeutic relationship in psychotherapy. State the ethical standards in psychotherapy. **(CBSE 2018)**

Ans. Psychotherapy is a voluntary relationship between the client (patient) and the therapist. The purpose of the relationship is to help the client to solve the psychological problems being faced by her or him.

Psychotherapies aim at changing the maladaptive behaviours, decreasing the sense of personal distress and helping the client to adapt better to her/his environment. Inadequate marital, occupational and social adjustment also require that major changes be made in an individual's personal environment.

The interactions between the therapist and the client results in the formation of therapeutic relationship. This is a confidential, interpersonal and dynamic relationship.

This human relationship is central to any type of psychotherapy. The ethical standards in psychotherapy should include

- Support client for attaining betterment.
- Lessening emotional pressure.
- Unfolding the potential for positive growth.
- Modifying habits.
- Changing thinking patterns.
- Increasing self-awareness.
- Improving interpersonal relations and communication.
- Facilitating decision-making.
- Becoming aware of one's choices in life.
- Relating to one's social environment in a more creative and self-aware manner.

2. What are the different types of psychotherapies? Explain the principles on which humanistic-existential therapy is based.

Ans. The different types of psychotherapies are as follows

   (i) **Behaviour Therapy** Behaviour therapies postulate that psychological distress arises because of faulty behaviour patterns or thought patterns. It is, therefore, focused on the behaviour and thoughts of the client in the present. The past is relevant only to the extent of understanding the origins of the faulty behaviour and thought patterns. Behaviour therapy consists of a large set of specific techniques and interventions.

   (ii) **Cognitive Therapy** Cognitive therapies locate the cause of psychological distress in irrational thoughts and beliefs. Albert Ellis formulated the Rational Emotive Therapy (RET). The central thesis of this therapy is that irrational beliefs mediate between the antecedent events and their consequences.

   (iii) **Humanistic–Existential Therapy** The humanistic-existential therapies claims that psychological distress arises from feelings of loneliness, alienation and an inability to find meaning and genuine fulfilment in life.

Principles of Humanistic-Existential Therapy The humanistic-existential therapy works on the principle of self-actualisation. Self-actualisation requires free emotional expression.

This therapy creates a permissive, non-judgemental and accepting atmosphere in which the client's emotions can be freely expressed and the complexity, balance and integration could be achieved.

3. Discuss the various techniques used in behaviour therapy.   **(NCERT, CBSE 2020)**

Ans. Various techniques which are used in behaviour therapy are as follows

- **Negative Reinforcement** It refers to following an undesired response with an outcome that is painful or not liked.

- **Aversive Conditioning** It refers to repeated association of undesired response with an aversive consequence.

- **Positive Reinforcement** If an adaptive behaviour occurs rarely, positive reinforcement is given to increase the deficit.

- **Token Economy** Person with behavioural problems can be given a token as a reward every time when a wanted behaviour occurs. The tokens are collected and exchanged for a reward such as an outing for the patient or a treat for the child. This is known as token economy.

- **Differential Reinforcement** Unwanted behaviour can be reduced and wanted behaviour can be increased simultaneously through differential reinforcement. Positive reinforcement for the wanted behaviour and negative reinforcement for the unwanted behaviour attempted together may be one such method. The other method is to positively reinforce the wanted behaviour and ignore the unwanted behaviour. The latter method is less painful and equally effective.

- **Systematic Desensitisation** It is a technique introduced by Wolpe for treating phobias or irrational fears. The client is interviewed to elicit fear-provoking situations. The therapist relaxes the client and asks the client to think about the least anxiety-provoking situation. The client is asked to stop thinking of the fearful situation if the slightest tension is felt.

- **Principle of Reciprocal Inhibition** This principle states that the presence of two mutually opposing forces at the same time inhibits the weaker force. Thus, the relaxation response is first built up and mildly anxiety-provoking scene is imagined, through which the anxiety is overcome by the relaxation. The client is able to tolerate progressively greater levels of anxiety because of her/his relaxed state.

- **Modelling** It is the procedure wherein the client learns to behave in a certain way by observing the behaviour of a role model or the therapist who initially acts as the role model.

4. How is Rational Emotive Therapy (RET) used in treating psychological disorders?

Or How does Rational Emotive Therapy help in reducing distress? Support your answer with the help of an example.   **(CBSE 2019)**

Or Explain the key features of cognitive therapies as explained by Albert Ellis.   **(CBSE 2020)**

Ans. Albert Ellis formulated the Rational Emotive Therapy (RET). The RET method helps in reducing psychological disorders in the followings ways

- The first step in RET is the Antecedent Belief-Consequence (ABC) analysis. Antecedent events, which caused the psychological distress, are noted.

- The client is also interviewed to find the irrational beliefs, which are distorting the present reality. Irrational beliefs may not be supported by empirical evidence in the environment. These beliefs are characterised by thoughts with 'musts' and 'shoulds', i.e. things 'must' and 'should' be in a particular manner.

- The distorted perception of the antecedent event due to the irrational belief leads to the consequence i.e. negative emotions and behaviours. For example, 'One should be loved by everybody all the time' is an irrational belief which leads to consequence of negative emotions and behaviours. Irrational beliefs are assessed through questionnaires and interviews. In the process of RET, the irrational beliefs are refuted by the therapist through a process of non-directive questioning.

- The questions make the client to think deeper into her/his assumptions about life and problems. Gradually, the client is able to change the irrational beliefs by making a change in her/his philosophy about life. The rational belief system replaces the irrational belief system and there is a reduction in psychological distress.

5. Explain psychological distress according to Humanist-Existential therapy. **(Delhi 2017)**

Or Describe four factors which contribute to treatment of psychological distress. **(All India 2017)**

Ans. **Humanistic-Existential** therapy claims that psychological distress arises from feelings of loneliness, alienation and an inability to find meaning and genuine fulfilment in life. Human beings are motivated by the desire for personal growth and self-actualisation and an innate need to grow emotionally. When these needs are controlled by society and family, individual experiences psychological distress.

Four factors which contribute to treatment of Psychological distress are as follows

(i) A major factor in the healing is the techniques adopted by the therapist and the implementation of the same with the patient/client. If the behavioural system and the CBT school are adopted to heal an anxious client, the relaxation procedures and the cognitive restructuring largely contribute to the healing.

(ii) The therapeutic alliance, which is formed between the therapist and the patient/client, has healing properties, because of the regular availability of the therapist and the warmth and empathy provided by the therapist.

(iii) At the beginning of therapy, while the patient/client is being interviewed in the initial sessions to understand the nature of the problem, she/he unburdens the emotional problems being faced. This process of emotional unburdening is known as **catharsis** and it has healing properties.

(iv) There are several non-specific factors associated with psychotherapy. Some of these factors are attributed to the patient/client and some to the therapist. Non-specific factors attributable (available) to the client/patient are motivation for change, expectation of improvement due to the treatment, etc. These are called **patient variables**. Non-specific factors attributable to the therapist are positive nature, absence of unresolved emotional conflicts, presence of good mental health, etc. These are called therapist variables.

6. Explain with examples that how cognitive distortions take place.

Or Explain cognitive distortion with the help of an example. **(CBSE 2019)**

Ans. Cognitive distortions are ways of thinking which are general in nature but which distort the reality in a negative manner. These patterns of thought are called dysfunctional cognitive structure. They lead to errors of cognition about the social reality. Psychological distress develops due to negative experiences provided by family and society. Individual develops negative thoughts like 'Nobody loves me', 'I am ugly', 'I am stupid', 'I will not succeed', etc. Such negative automatic thoughts are characterised by cognitive distortions.

Repeated occurrence of these thoughts lead to the development of feelings of anxiety and depression. The therapist uses questioning which is gentle non-threatening disputation of the client's beliefs and thoughts. The therapist asks him 'why should everyone love you', or 'what does it mean to you to succeed'?

The question makes the client think in a direction opposite to that of the negative automatic thoughts. He gains insight into the nature of his dysfunctional schemas and is able to alter his cognitive structure. The aim of this therapy is to achieve this cognitive restructuring which in turn reduces anxiety and depression.

7. What is rehabilitation? What are the techniques used in the rehabilitation of the mentally ill?

Ans. Rehabilitation is required to help patients become self-sufficient. The aim of rehabilitation is to empower the patient to become a productive member of society to the extent possible.

In rehabilitation, the patients are given occupational therapy, social skills training and vocational therapy. The techniques used in the rehabilitation of the mentally ill are Occupation Therapy, Social Skill Training, Cognitive Ritraining and Vocational Training. These are discussed as follows

- **Occupational Therapy** In this therapy, the patients are taught skills such as candle making, paper bag making and weaving to help them to form a work discipline.
- **Social Skills Training** It helps the patients to develop interpersonal skills through role play, imitation and instruction. The objective is to teach the patient to function in a social group.
- **Cognitive Retraining** It is given to improve the basic cognitive functions of attention, memory and executive functions.
- **Vocational Training** When the patient becomes self-sufficient vocational training is given wherein the patient is helped to gain skills necessary to undertake employment.

• Case Based Questions

1. Lovleen is a 10-year old teenage girl who cries and refuses to talk (sulk) when she is not taken to the cinema. Her mother, who is a teacher, came across a psychological technique for handling such behaviour in a parenting book. Lovleen's parents took her to the cinema if she did not cry and sulk. However, if Lovleen cried and sulked, her parents simply ignored her and did not take her to the cinema.

Gradually, the wanted behaviour of politely asking to be taken to the cinema increased and the unwanted behaviour of crying and sulking decreased. This in fact helped to improve Lovleen's overall behaviour of sulking for everything. She eventually learnt that asking for things politely is much better way of behaving than sulking for everything.

(i) What behavioural technique has been used by Lovleen's parents in the passage?

Ans. The behavioural technique used in the given example is called differential reinforcement. As per this technique unwanted behaviour can be reduced and wanted behaviour can be increased simultaneously through differential reinforcement.

(ii) Name all the behavioural techniques. Explain at least one in detail.

Ans. Following are the behavioural techniques:
- Positive reinforcement
- Aversive conditioning
- Differential reinforcement
- Token economy
- Negative reinforcement
- Systematic desensitisation
- Modelling
- Principle of Reciprocal Inhibition

Modelling It is the procedure wherein the client learns to behave in a certain way by observing the behaviour of a role model or the therapist who initially acts as the role model.

(iii) Lovleen is given a token every time she behaves in a desired way? What is this technique called? Explain it in detail.

Ans. This technique is known as token economy. Person with behavioural problems can be given a token as a reward every time when a wanted behaviour occurs. The tokens are collected and exchanged for a reward such as an outing for the patient or a treat for the child.

Chapter Test

Multiple Choice Questions

1. Who introduced systematic desensitisation technique?
  (a) Carl Jung (b) Wolpe
  (c) Laura Peris (d) Fritz

2. The stage of transference in which the therapist becomes a substitute for the person in present is known as
  (a) Transference neurosis (b) Transference neurons
  (c) Transference process (d) Transference therapist

3. The inborn force that forces a person to become more balanced is known as
  (a) Self-realisation (b) Self-perception
  (c) Self-actualisation (d) Self-acknowledgement

4. The goal of _____ is to increase an individual's self-awareness and self-acceptance.
  (a) Gestalt Therapy (b) Client-Centred Therapy
  (c) Logotherapy (d) None of these

5. _____ is the procedure wherein the client learns to behave in a certain way by observing the behaviour of a role model or the therapist who initially acts as the role model.
  (a) Token Economy (b) Aversive Conditioning
  (c) Modelling (d) All of these

Short Answer Type Questions

4. Define psychotherapy.

5. What are the aims of psychotherapies?

6. What do you mean by alliance?

7. Define modelling.

8. Explain the technique of token money.

Long Answer Type Questions

9. Discuss methodology used in behaviour therapy.

10. Describe modality of psychoanalysis as a therapy.

11. How can we formulate a client's problems?

Answers

1. (b) *2.* (a) *3.* (c) *4.* (a) *5.* (c)

CHAPTER 03

Attitude and Social Cognition

In this Chapter...

Introduction

Social psychology is that branch of psychology which investigates how the behaviour of an individual is affected by others and the social environment. All of us form attitudes or ways of thinking about specific topics and people. We also form impressions about persons we meet and assign causes to their behaviour. Besides, our own behaviour gets influenced by other individuals and groups. In some situations, people show pro-social behaviour, that is, helping the needy and the distressed, without expecting anything in return. Many of these social behaviours seem to be simple. Yet, explaining the processes that lie behind these behaviours is a complex matter.

Social Behaviour

Social behaviour is a necessary part of human life. It is much more than just being in the company of others. Our social environment influences our **thoughts, emotions** and **behaviour** in complex ways. Social psychologists examine various forms of social behaviour and try to explain their basis. Due to social influences, people form **views** or attitudes about people and different issues that exist in the form of behavioural tendencies.

Impression formation happens when we meet people and make conclusion about their personal qualities. We also assign causes to the behaviour shown in specific social situations and this process is known as **attribution**. Impression formation, attributions, attitudes–these three processes are collectively called **social cognition**. Social cognition is activated by cognitive units called **schemas**.

Cognitive processes cannot be directly seen. They have to be inferred on the basis of an externally shown behaviour. There are other examples of social influence that are in the form of observable behaviour. Two such examples are, social facilitation/inhibition i.e. the improvement or decline in performance in the presence of others. **Pro-social behaviour** is responding to others who are in need or distress. In order to understand how the social context influences the individual, it is necessary to study both social-cognitive process and social behaviour.

Social psychologists suggest that one must go beyond common sense and folk wisdom to explain how people observe and understand their own and others' behaviour. To explain social behaviour we have to adopt scientific methods and systematic-objective observations.

In order to understand completely how the social context influences the individual, it is necessary to study both social-cognitive processes and social behaviour. Through systematic and objective observations and by adopting scientific methods, it is possible to establish logical cause and effect relationships that explain social behaviour.

Nature and Components of Attitude

An attitude is a state of the mind, a set of views or thoughts, regarding some topic (called the 'attitude object'), which have an evaluative feature (positive, negative or neutral quality). It is accompanied by an emotional component and a tendency to act in a particular way with regard to the attitude object. If our views are not merely thoughts, but also have emotional and action components, then these views are the examples of attitudes.

Components of an Attitude

The thought component is referred to as the **cognitive aspect**, the emotional component is known as the **affective aspect** and the tendency to act is called the **behavioural** (or conative) **aspect**. These three aspects have been referred to as the A-B-C components i.e. Affective-Behavioural and Cognitive components of attitude.

For example, suppose a group of people in your neighbourhood start a tree plantation campaign as part of a 'green environment' movement. Based on sufficient information about the environment, your view towards a 'green environment' is positive (cognitive or 'C' component, along with the evaluative aspect). You feel very happy when you see greenery.

You feel sad and angry when you see trees being cut down. These aspects reflect the affective (emotional) or 'A' component of the same attitude. Now suppose you also actively participate in the tree plantation campaign. This shows the behavioural or 'B' component of your attitudes towards a 'green environment'.

In general, we expect all three components to be consistent with each other, that is, in the same direction. Predicting one component on the basis of the other two may not always give us the correct picture about an attitude.

Beliefs and Values

Attitudes have to be distinguished from two other closely related concepts, namely beliefs and values. Beliefs refer to the cognitive component of attitudes and form the ground on which attitudes stand, such as belief in God or belief in democracy as a political ideology. Values are attitudes or beliefs that contain a 'should' or 'ought' aspect, such as moral or ethical values. For example, one should work hard or one should be honest.

Values are formed when a particular belief or attitude becomes an inseparable part of the person's outlook on life. Consequently, values are difficult to change.

Features of an Attitude

Attitudes provide a background that makes it easier for a person to decide how to act in new situations. In addition to the affective, cognitive and behavioural components, attitudes also have other properties. Four significant features of attitudes are as follows

1. Valence (Positivity or Negativity)

The valence of an attitude tells us whether an attitude is positive or negative towards the attitude object. A neutral attitude would have neither positive nor negative valence.

For example, an attitude towards nuclear research has to be expressed on a 5 point scale, ranging from 1 (very bad), 2 (bad), 3 (neutral-neither good nor bad), 4 (good) and 5 (very good). If an individual rates his view as 1, 2 then it is negative attitude, if he rates 4 to 5 then it is positive attitude and if he rates 3 then it is neutral attitude i.e. neither positive nor negative valence.

2. Extremeness

The **extremeness of an attitude** indicates how positive or negative an attitude is. For example, if an individual rates the nuclear research as 1 or 5, these are regarded as extreme ratings. They are only in the opposite directions (valence). A neutral attitude is lowest on extremeness.

3. Simplicity or Complexity (Multiplicity)

This feature refers to how many attitudes are there within a broader attitude. In case of various topics, such as health and world peace, people hold many attitudes instead of single attitude. An attitude system is said to be simple if it contains only one or a few attitudes and complex if it is made up of many attitudes. The attitude towards a particular person is likely to consist of mainly one attitude.

The multiple member-attitudes within an attitude system should not be confused with the three components described as A-B-C components.

4. Centrality

This refers to the role of a particular attitude in the attitude system. An attitude with higher centrality would have a larger impact on other attitudes (non-central attitudes).

For example, in the attitude towards world peace, a negative attitude towards high military expenditure may be present as a core or central attitude. This influences all attitudes in the multiple attitude system.

Attitude Formation and Change

Attitudes towards different topics, things and people are formed as we interact with others. However, there are specific conditions that lead to the formation of specific attitudes. In general, attitudes are learned through one's own experiences and through interaction with others.

Process of Attitude Formation

The processes and conditions of learning may be different, resulting in varying attitudes among people. Various process of attitude formation are as follows

Learning Attitudes by Association

You might have seen that students often develop a liking for a particular subject because of the positive qualities in that teacher. These positive qualities get linked to the subject that she/he teaches and ultimately get expressed in the form of liking for the subject. In other words, a positive attitude towards the subject is learned through the positive association between a teacher and a student.

Learning Attitudes by Being Rewarded or Punished

If an individual is praised for showing a particular attitude, chances are high that she/he will develop that attitude further. For example, if a teenager does yogasanas regularly and gets the honour of being 'Miss Good Health' in her school, she may develop a positive attitude towards yoga and health in general.

Similarly, if a child frequently falls ill because of his intake of junk food instead of proper meals, gradually he develops a negative attitude towards junk food and positive attitude towards healthy meal.

Learning Attitudes through Modelling (Observing Others)

We learn attitudes by observing others being rewarded or punished for expressing thoughts or showing behaviour of a particular kind towards the attitude object. For example, children may form a respectful attitude towards elders, by observing that their parents show respect for elders and are appreciated for it.

Learning Attitudes through Group or Cultural Norms

We learn attitudes through the norms of our group or culture. Norms are unwritten rules about behaviour that everyone is supposed to show under specific circumstances.

Over time, these norms may become part of our social cognition in the form of attitudes. For example, offering money, sweets, fruit and flowers in a place of worship is a normative behaviour in some religions.

When individual sees that such behaviour is socially approved, he may develop a positive attitude towards such behaviour and the associated feelings of devotion.

Learning through Exposure to Information

Many attitudes are learned in a social context, but not necessarily in the physical presence of others. Today, with the huge amount of information that is being provided through various media, both positive and negative attitudes are being formed.

By reading the biographies of **self-actualised persons**[1], an individual may develop a positive attitude towards hard work and other aspects as the means of achieving success in life.

Factors that Influence Attitude Formation

The following factors influence the learning of attitudes

1. Family and School Environment

Family and the school environment play a significant role in shaping attitude formation.

Learning of attitudes within the family and school usually takes place by association, through rewards and punishments and through modelling.

2. Reference Groups

It indicates to an individual the norms regarding acceptable behaviour and ways of thinking. Thus, they reflect learning of attitudes through group or cultural norms. Attitudes towards various topics, such as political, religious and social groups, occupations, national and other issues are often developed through reference groups.

Their influence is noticeable especially during the beginning of adolescence, at which time it is important for the individual to feel that she/he belongs to a group. Therefore, the role of reference groups in attitude formation may also be a case of learning through reward and punishment.

3. Personal Experiences

Many attitudes are formed through direct personal experiences which bring about a drastic change in our attitude towards people and our own life.

For example, a driver in army escaped death in an accident where all his companions got killed. After that he left the job and became a community leader for the upliftment of his community.

---

1 **Self-actualised Persons** These are those persons who accept themselves and others as they are.

4. Media-related Influences

Technological advances in recent times have made audio-visual media and the Internet very powerful sources of information that lead to attitude formation and change. In addition, school level textbooks also influence attitude formation. These sources first strengthen the cognitive and affective components of attitudes and gradually may affect the behavioural component.

The media can apply both good and bad influences on attitudes. The media can be used to create consumerist attitude where it does not exist. It can also create positive attitudes to facilitate social harmony.

Attitude Change

During and after the process of attitude formation, attitudes may be changed and modified through various influences. Attitudes that are still in the formative stage, are much more likely to change compared to attitudes that have become firmly established and have become a part of the individual's values.

Process of Attitude Change

Three major concepts of processes in attitude change are described as follows

1. The Concept of Balance

It was proposed by **Fritz Heider**. It is also described in the form of the **P-O-X** triangle, which represents the relationships between three aspects or components of the attitude.

- P is the person whose attitude is being studied.
- O is another person.
- X is the topic towards which the attitude is being studied (attitude object).

Consider the example of dowry as an attitude topic (X). A person has a positive attitude toward dowry (P-X positive). P is planning to get his son married to the daughter of some person O. O has a negative attitude towards dowry (O-X negative).

If O initially has a positive attitude towards P, the situation would be unbalanced. P-X is positive, O-P is positive but O-X is negative. This situation is a situation of imbalance. One of the three attitudes will have to change to make the situation as a situation of balance.

It is also possible that all three are persons. An attitude changes if there is a state of imbalance between the P-O attitude, O-X attitude and P-X attitude because imbalance is logically uncomfortable.

Therefore, the attitude changes in the direction of balance. Imbalance is found when all three sides of the P-O-X triangle are negative or two sides are positive, and one side is

negative. Balance is found when all three sides are positive or two sides are negative and one side is positive.

2. The Concept of Cognitive Dissonance

It was proposed by **Leon Festinger**. It emphasises that the cognitive components of an attitude must be consonant (opposite of dissonant) i.e. they should be logically in line with each other.

Festinger and **Carlsmith**, two social psychologists, conducted an experiment that showed the working of **cognitive dissonance**[2]. Both balance and cognitive dissonance are examples of cognitive consistency.

Cognitive consistency means that two components, aspects or elements of the attitude or attitude system, must be in the same direction. Each element should logically fall in line with other elements.

If this does not happen, then the person experiences a kind of mental discomfort i.e. the sense that 'something is not quite right'. In such a state, some aspect in the attitude system changes in the direction of consistency, because our cognitive system requires logical consistency.

3. The Two-Step Concept

It was proposed by **SM Mohsin**, an Indian psychologist. According to him, attitude change takes place in the form of two steps. These are as follows

(i) **In the first step**, the target of change identifies with the source. The target is the person whose attitude is to be changed. The source is the person through whose influence the change is to take place. Identification means that the target has liking and regard for the source. The source must also have a positive attitude towards the target and the regard and attraction becomes mutual.

(ii) **In the second step**, the source herself/himself shows an attitude change, by actually changing her/his behaviour towards the attitude object. Observing the source's changed attitude and behaviour, the target also shows an attitude change through behaviour. This is a kind of imitation or observational learning.

Factors that Influence Attitude Change

Following are the major factors that influence attitude change

Characteristics of the Existing Attitude

All four features i.e. valence (Positivity and Negativity), extremeness, simplicity and centrality of attitudes determine attitude change. In general, positive attitudes are easier to change than negative attitudes. Extreme attitudes and central attitudes are more difficult to change than the less extreme and peripheral (less significant) attitudes. Simple attitudes are easier to change than multiple attitudes.

---

2 Cognitive Dissonance It refers to the mental conflict that occurs when a person's behaviours and beliefs do not align.

An attitude change may be congruent (favourable), it may change in the same direction as the existing attitude (for example, a positive attitude may become more positive or a negative attitude may become more negative).

On the other hand, an attitude change may be **incongruent** (incompatible). It may change in a direction opposite to the existing attitude (for example, a positive attitude becomes less positive/negative or a negative attitude becomes less negative/positive). Moreover, an attitude may change in the direction of the information that is presented or in a direction opposite to that of the information presented.

Source Characteristics

Source credibility and attractiveness are two features that affect attitude change. Attitudes are more likely to change when the message comes from a highly credible source rather than from a low-credible source.

For example, a person wants to buy a laptop will be more convinced to hear recommendation from a computer engineer than a school child who gives the same information.

Message Characteristics

The message is the information that is presented in order to bring about an attitude change. Attitudes will change when the amount of information that is given about the topic is just enough, neither too much nor too little.

Whether the meassage contains a **rational** or an **emotional appeal** makes a difference. For example, an advertisement for cooking food in a pressure cooker may point out that this saves fuel and it is economical. The motives activated by the message determine attitude change.

For example, drinking milk may be said to make a person healthy, good looking, energetic and successful. The **mode** of spreading the message plays a significant role. The benefits of taking ORS spread through visual media like posters, advertisement on television, etc.

Face-to-face transmission of the message is usually more effective than indirect transmission i.e. through letters and pamphlets or even through mass media.

Target Characteristics

Qualities of the target, such as persuasibility, strong prejudices, self-esteem and intelligence influence the likelihood and extent of an attitude change.

People who have a more open and flexible personality, change more easily. People with strong preconceptions are less prone or inclined to any attitude change.

Persons who have a low self-esteem and do not have sufficient confidence in themselves, change their attitudes more easily than those who are high on self-esteem.

More intelligent people may change their attitudes less easily than those with lower intelligence. However, sometimes more intelligent persons change their attitudes more willingly than less intelligent ones, because they base their attitude on more information and thinking.

Relationship between Attitude and Behaviour

An individual's attitudes may not always be exhibited through behaviour. One's actual behaviour may be contrary to one's attitude towards a particular topic. Attitudes may not always predict actual pattern of one's behaviour. Sometimes, it is behaviour that decides the attitude.

Psychologists have found that there would be consistency between attitudes and behaviour when

- The attitude is strong and occupies a central place in the attitude system.
- The person is aware of her/his attitude.
- There is very little or no external pressure for the person to behave in a particular way.
- The person's behaviour is not being watched or evaluated by others.
- The person thinks that the behaviour would have a positive consequence and therefore, intends to engage in that behaviour.

Prejudice and Discrimination

Prejudices are examples of attitudes towards a particular group. They are usually negative and in many cases, may be based on **stereotypes** (the cognitive component) about the specific group. A stereotype is a cluster of ideas regarding the characteristics of a specific group. Stereotypes consist of undesirable characteristics about the target group and they lead to negative attitudes or prejudices towards members of specific groups.

Prejudice may also grow as discrimination but prejudices can exist without showing discrimination. Similarly, **discrimination**[3] can be shown without prejudice. Wherever prejudice and discrimination exist, conflicts are very likely to arise between groups within the same society.

---

3 Discrimination It is the behaviour that shows a distinction being made between two or more persons often on the basis of the person's (or person's) membership of a particular group.

For example, the genocide committed by the Nazis in Germany against Jewish people is an example of how prejudice can lead to hatred, discrimination and mass killing of innocent prople. We get numerous examples from history containing discrimination based on race and caste on social class.

Social psychologists have shown that prejudice has the following sources

- **Learning** Like other attitudes, prejudices can also be learned through association, reward and punishment, observing others, group or cultural norms and exposure to information that encourages prejudice. The family, reference groups, personal experiences and the media may play a role in the learning of prejudices.
  People who learn prejudiced attitudes may develop a 'prejudiced personality' and show low adjusting capacity, anxiety and feelings of hostility against the outgroup.
- **A Strong Social Identity and Ingroup Bias** Individuals who have a strong sense of social identity and have a very positive attitude towards their own group boost this attitude by holding negative attitudes towards other groups. These are shown as prejudices.
- **Scapegoating** This is a phenomenon by which the majority group places the blame on a minority outgroup for its own social, economic or political problems. The minority is too weak or too small in number to defend itself against such accusations (complaints). Scapegoating is a group based way of expressing frustration and it often results in negative attitudes or prejudice against the weaker group.
- **Kernel of Truth Concept** Sometimes people may continue to hold stereotypes because they think that there must be some truth or 'kernel of truth' in what everyone says about the other group.

- **Self-fulfilling Prophecy** In some cases, the group that is the target of prejudice is itself responsible for continuing the prejudice. The target group may behave in ways that justify the prejudice i.e. confirm the negative expectations.

For example, if the target group is described as 'dependent' and therefore unable to make progress. The members of this target group may actually behave in a way that proves this description to be true.

Strategies for Handling Prejudice

The first step in handling prejudice is to know about its causes or sources. Thus, the strategies for handling prejudice would be effective if they aim at

- Minimising opportunities for learning prejudices.
- Changing prejudice attitudes.
- De-emphasising a narrow social identity based on the ingroup.
- Discouraging the tendency towards self-fulfilling prophecy among the victims of prejudice.

These goals can be accomplished through

- Education and information dissemination, for correcting stereotypes related to specific target groups and tackling the problem of a strong ingroup bias.
- Increasing intergroup contact helps to have more communication between different groups, helps to reduce any feelings of mistrust and also helps to discover positive aspects of different groups.
  These strategies are successful only if
  - The two groups meet in a cooperative rather than competitive context.
  - Close interactions between the groups helps them to know each other better.
  - The two groups are not different in power or status.
- Highlighting individual identity rather than group identity, which weaken the importance of group (both ingroup and outgroup) as a basis of evaluating the other person.

Chapter Practice

Objective Questions

• Multiple Choice Questions

1. Performance on specific tasks is influenced by the mere presence of others. This is called
(a) Social facilitation (b) Social obligation
(c) Social norm (d) Social attribution

Ans. (a) Performance on specific tasks is influenced by the mere presence of others called social facilitation. Social facilitation refers to impact posed by presence of people on a person's behaviours.

2. An augmentation in behaviour due to the presence of other individuals is known as
(a) Imitation (b) Social facilitation
(c) Interaction (d) None of the above

Ans. (b) An augmentation in behaviour due to the presence of other individuals is known as Social facilitation .

3. What indicates the degree of how positive or negative an attitude is?
(a) Extremeness (b) Simplicity
(c) Centrality (d) Valence

Ans. (a) It is extremeness of an attitude that indicates how positive or negative an attitude is.

4. Shashi has a score of 5 in her behaviour. Her behaviour is
(a) Neutral (b) Extreme (c) Average (d) Moderate

Ans. (b) Shashi's behaviour is extreme. The extremeness of an attitude indicates how positive or negative an attitude is.

5. __________attitude is lowest on extremeness.
(a) Positive (b) Negative (c) Neutral (d) Happy

Ans. (c) A Neutral attitude is lowest on extremeness.

6. Which of the following influences your attitude?
(a) Media (b) Parents
(c) School (d) All of these

Ans. (d) Media, parents and schools are the factors that influence our attitude.

7. There was a marriage in which dowry was being given. Ramesh is the groom and does not want dowry. Sunita is the bride who is giving the dowry. As per P-O-X triangle, what can be denoted as O.
(a) Ramesh (b) Sunita
(c) Dowry (d) None

Ans. (c) As per P-O-X triangle. Dowry can be denoted as O.

8. In 1957, Leon Festinger published his theory of
(a) Balance
(b) Cognitive Dissonance
(c) Attribution
(d) None of the above

Ans. (b) Leon Festinger published his theory of Cognitive dissonance in 1957.

9. Students often develop a liking for a particular subject because of the teacher. This liking is because of
(a) Positive association between a teacher and a student
(b) Negative association between a teacher and a student
(c) Neutral association between a teacher and a student
(d) Both (a) and (b)

Ans. (a) This liking is because of Positive association between a teacher and a student.

10. Two-step concept was proposed by________.
(a) Sigmund Freud (b) Ivan Pavlov
(c) SM Mohsin (d) Fritz Heider

Ans. (c) The two-step concept was proposed by SM Mohsin, an Indian psychologist.

11. Which among the following influences attitude change?
1. Characteristics of the Existing Attitude
2. Characteristic of the attitude of other people
3. Source Characteristics
4. Target Characteristic

Choose the correct option
(a) 1,2,3 (b) 2,3 (c) 1,3,4 (d) 2,4

Ans. (c) The factors that influences attitude change are Characteristics of the Existing Attitude, Source Characteristics and Target Characteristic.

12. Which of the following is true about prejudices and discrimination?

1. Prejudices are examples of attitudes towards a particular group.
2. They are usually negative and in many cases, may be based on stereotypes.
3. Prejudice may also grow as discrimination.
4. Prejudices cannot exist without showing discrimination.

Choose the correct option

(a) 1,2,3   (b) 2,3
(c) 1,3,4   (d) 2,4

Ans. (a) Prejudices generally refer to an attitude developed for a particular group of people. Such an attitude is generally negative and in many cases may be based on stereotypes. Prejudice may also grow as discrimination.

13. Cluster of ideas regarding the characteristics of a specific group is known as

(a) Progressive
(b) Stereotype
(c) Belief
(d) Attitude

Ans. (b) A stereotype is a cluster of ideas regarding the characteristics of a specific group.

14. Which of the following statements are true about prejudice and discrimination?

1. Prejudice may also grew as discrimination.
2. Discrimination can be shown without prejudice.
3. Conflicts are likely to arise between groups and in same society wherever prejudice and discrimination exist.
4. Prejudice can not exist without shown discrimination

Choose the correct options

(a) 1, 2, 3
(b) 2, 3, 4
(c) 1, 2, 4
(d) 2, 4, 1

Ans. (a) Statements 1, 2, 3 are true but statement 4 is not true as Prejudice can exist without shown discrimination. Thus, correct option is (a).

15. Tarun's group has won the elections from his constituency. His opponents, Ramesh and his group, are weak and too small in number. Tarun often expresses frustration and negative attitude towards Ramesh's group. This is known as __________.

(a) Learning
(b) Kernel of truth concept
(c) Scapegoating
(d) Imitation

Ans. (a) This is known as scapegoating. It is the group based way of expressing frustration and negative attitude.

• Assertion-Reasoning MCQs

Direction (Q. Nos. 1-4) *Each of these questions contains two statements, Assertion (A) and Reason (R). Each of these questions also has four alternative choices, any one of which is the correct answer. You have to select one of the codes (a), (b), (c) and (d) given below.*

(a) Both A and R are true and R is the correct explanation of A
(b) Both A and R are true but R is not the correct explanation of A
(c) A is True and R is false
(d) A is false and R is true

1. Assertion (A) Centrality refers to the role of a particular attitude in the attitude system.

Reason (R) An attitude with greater centrality would influence the other attitudes in the system much more than non-central (or peripheral) attitudes.

Ans. (a) Both A and R are true and R is the correct explanation of A. Centrality refers to the role of a particular attitude in the attitude system. A central attitude is thought to influence the other attitudes in the system much more than non-central attitudes. This influences all attitudes in the multiple attitude system. Hence, R correctly explains A.

2. Assertion (A) Reference groups are the norms regarding acceptable behaviour and ways of thinking.

Reason (R) A person's attitude development for certain topics often occurs as per these norms.

Ans. (a) Both A and R are true and R is the correct explanation of A. Reference groups are the norms regarding acceptable behaviour and ways of thinking. Thus, A person's attitude towards various topics, such as political, religious and social groups, are ofter developed as per these norms.

3. Assertion (A) Qualities of the target influence attitude change.

Reason (R) People who are more flexible do not change more easily.

Ans. (c) Qualities of the target, such as persuasibility, strong prejudices, self-esteem and intelligence influence the attitude change. People who are more open and flexible change more easily. People with strong preconceptions are less prone or inclined to any attitude change. Hence, A is true and R is false.

4. Assertion (A) Attitude is strong and occupies a central place in the attitude system.

Reason (R) One's actual behaviour may be contrary to one's attitude towards a particular topic.

Ans. (b) Both A and R are true and R is not the correct explanation of A. Attitude is strong and occupies a central place in attitude system. One's actual behaviour maybe differ from one's attitude towards particular thing. R do not explain A.

• Case Based MCQs

1. Tanya is a mother of two boys. One of her boys, Varun, had been complaining of a stomach ache lately. Tanya took Varun to the doctor. Doctor prescribed a few painkillers along with an antibiotic. However, Tanya had a strong belief that antibiotics do not work and can lead to serious side effects. This mindset of Tanya's developed because of the penicillin allergy that her best friend has. So Tanya did not give antibiotics to Varun. Sadly, Varun's condition did not improve and eventually deteriorated. When doctors questioned Tanya about the medicine consumption Tanya admitted that she did not give Varun the prescribed antibiotics. Hence, Tanya was scolded badly by the doctor and she eventually gave antibiotics to Varun. Varun's condition thereafter improved.

(i) As per the P-O-X who is denoted as P.
   (a) Tanya
   (b) Doctor
   (c) Varun
   (d) Antibiotics use
   Ans (a) As per the P-O-X Tanya is denoted as P.

(ii) Imbalance is found when______ .
   (a) All three sides of the P-O-X triangle are negative
   (b) Two sides are positive
   (c) One side is negative
   (d) All of the above
   Ans (d) Imbalance is found in all the given options.

(iii) Balance of attitude is found in which condition?
   (a) All three sides are negative
   (b) Two sides are negative
   (c) Two sides are positive
   (d) All three sides of the P-O-X triangle are negative
   Ans (b) When two sides are negative balance of attitude is found.

(iv) The attitude change always occur in the direction of
   (a) Balance
   (b) Imbalance
   (c) Any direction
   (d) It does not change
   Ans (a) The attitude change always occurs in the direction of balance.

(v) Which of the following is incorrect?
   (a) It is also possible that all three components of the P-O-X triangle are persons
   (b) Attitude changes because imbalance is comfortable
   (c) Other name for P-O-X triangle is concept of balance
   (d) It was given by Fritz Heider
   Ans (b) Attitude changes because imbalance is comfortable is not correct.

(vi) **Assertion** (A) Changing the attitude of Tanya towards antibiotics was difficult.
   Reason (R) This belief had been there since a while and the attitude had become firm.
   Codes
   (a) Both A and R are true and R is the correct explanation of A
   (b) Both A and R are true, but R is not the correct explanation of A
   (c) A is true, but R is false
   (d) R is true, but A is false
   Ans (a) Both A and R are true, R is the correct explanation for A. As changing in attitude of tanya was difficult Attitudes that are still in the formative stage, are much more likely to change compared to attitudes that have become firmly established and have become a part of the individual's values.

PART 2
Subjective Questions

• Short Answer (SA) Type Questions

1. Define attitude. Discuss the components of an attitude.   **(NCERT)**

Or What is attitude. Explain its various components.   **(CBSE 2020)**

Ans. An attitude is a state of the mind, a set of views or thoughts, regarding some topics (called the 'attitude object'), which have an evaluative feature (positive, negative or neutral quality).

Attitude have three components. These are as follows

(i) The thought component is referred to as the cognitive aspect. It consists of belief, ideas, values and other information that a person may possess or has faith in. It makes little difference if the information is correct or incorrect.

(ii) The emotional component is known as the affective aspect. It is related to person's feelings about another person, which may be positive, negative or neutral.

(iii) The tendency to act is called the behavioural (or cognative) aspect. It is related to impact of various situations or objects that lead to individual's behaviour based on cognitive and affective components. Only this component of attitude is visible.

2. Distinguish between belief and values.

Ans. The difference between belief and values are as follows

	Belief	Values
(i)	Beliefs refer to cognitive component of attitudes and form the grounds on which the attitudes form such as belief in god.	Values are attitudes or beliefs that contain the 'should be' or 'ought to' factor.
(ii)	Belief can be changed more easily.	Values are inseparable part of a person's life and hence, are difficult to change.
(iii)	Beliefs are concepts that we hold to be true.	Values are ideas that hold to be important.

3. Discuss the four significant features of attitude.
(NCERT)

Ans. Four significant features of attitudes are as follows

(i) **Valence (Positivity or Negativity)** The valence of an attitude tells us whether an attitude is positive or negative towards the attitude object. A neutral attitude would have neither positive nor negative valence.

(ii) **Extremeness** The extremeness of an attitude indicates how positive or negative an attitude is. They are only in the opposite directions (valence). A neutral attitude is lowest on extremeness.

(iii) **Simplicity or Complexity (Multiplicity)** This feature refers to how many attitudes are there within a broader attitude. In case of various topics, such as health and world peace, people hold many attitudes instead of single attitude. An attitude system is said to be simple if it contains only one or a few attitudes, and complex if it is made up of many attitudes.

(iv) **Centrality** This refers to the role of a particular attitude in the attitude system. An attitude with greater centrality would influence the other attitudes in the system much more than non-central (or peripheral) attitudes.

4. Discuss how media can influence the attitude change.

Ans. In today's modern era media can influence the attitude change. Technological advances in recent times have made audio-visual media and the internet very powerful sources of information that lead to attitude formation and change.

These sources first strengthen the cognitive and affective components of attitudes, and subsequently may also affect the behavioural component. The media can exert both good and bad influences on attitudes. On one hand, the media and internet make people better informed than other modes of communication. They are also gradually becoming stronger in guiding public opinion. On the other hand, there may be no check on the nature of information being provided.

5. Discuss the concept of balance in attitude change.

Ans. Concept of balance was proposed by Fritz Heider. It is also described in the form of the 'P-O-X' triangle, which represents the relationships between three aspects or components of the attitude.

P is the person whose attitude is being studied, O is another person and X is the topic towards which the attitude is being studied (attitude object). It is also possible that all three are persons.

An attitude changes if there is a state of imbalance between the P-O attitude, O-X attitude, and P-X attitude because imbalance is logically uncomfortable.

Therefore, the attitude changes in the direction of balance. Imbalance is found when all three sides of the P-O-X triangle are negative, or two sides are positive, and one side is negative.

Balance is found when all three sides are positive, or two sides are negative, and one side is positive.

6. Discuss cognitive dissonance component in attitude change process.

Ans. Cognitive dissonance was proposed by Leon Festinger. It emphasises that the cognitive components of an attitude must be 'consonant' (opposite of dissonant) i.e. they should be logically in line with each other.

Festinger and Carlsmith, two social psychologists, conducted an experiment that showed the working of cognitive dissonance. Both balance and cognitive dissonance are examples of cognitive consistency.

Cognitive consistency means that two components, aspects or elements of the attitude, or attitude system, must be in the same direction. Each element should logically fall in line with other elements.

If this does not happen, then the person experiences a kind of mental discomfort. In such a state, some aspecsts in the attitude system changes in the direction of consistency, because our cognitive system requires logical consistency.

7. Discuss the attitude-behaviour relationship.

Ans. An individual's attitude may not always be exhibited through behaviour. One's actual behaviour may be contrary to one's attitude towards a particular topic.

Attitudes may not always predict actual pattern of one's behaviour. Sometimes, it is behaviour that decides the attitude. Psychologists have found that there would be consistency between attitudes and behaviour when

Following are some important points of attitude behaviour relationship

- The attitude is strong, and occupies a central place in the attitude system.
- The person is aware of her/his attitude.
- There is very little or no external pressure for the person to behave in a particular way.
- The person's behaviour is not being watched or evaluated by others.
- The person thinks that the behaviour would have a positive consequence, and therefore, intends to engage in that behaviour.

8. Prejudice can exist without discrimination and *vice versa*. Comment. **(NCERT)**

Ans. Prejudices can exist without being shown in the form of discrimination. Similarly, discrimination can be shown without prejudice. Yet, the two go together very often.

Wherever, prejudice and discrimination exist, conflicts are very likely to arise between groups within the same society.

Our own society has witnessed many deplorable instances of discrimination, with and without prejudice based on gender, religion, community, caste, physical handicap, and illnesses such as AIDS.

Moreover, in many cases discriminatory behaviour can be curbed by law. But, the cognitive and emotional components of prejudice are more difficult to change.

9. How do you explain prejudice and discrimination in the genocide committed by the Nazis in Germany against the Jewish people?

Ans. Prejudices are examples of attitudes towards a particular group. These are usually negative in nature. Sometimes these are based on stereotypes. Stereotype is an overgeneralised and unverified prototype about a particular group. It is a cluster of ideas regarding the characteristics of a specific group. All members belonging to this group are assumed to possesses these characteristics.

In Nazi Germany Jews remained the worst sufferers. Jews had been stereotyped as killers of Christ and money lenders. Jews lived in separately marked areas called 'ghettos'. They were persecuted through periodic organised violence and expulsion from the land. In Nazism the Jews were terrorised, pauperised and segregated. Large scale genocide was committed by the Nazis against the Jews.

This is an extreme example of how prejudice can lead to hatred, discrimination and mass killing of innocent people. The cognitive component of prejudice is accompanied by dislike or hatred generally. Thus,

prejudice may transformed into discrimination. Here, people behave in a less positive way toward a particular group than others. Exactly this was happened in Nazi Germany where prejudice and discrimination led to mass killings of innocent Jewish people.

10. Differentiate between prejudice and stereotype. **(NCERT)**

Ans. The difference between prejudice and stereotype are as follows

	Prejudice	Stereotype
(i)	Prejudices are example of attitudes towards a particular group. They are usually negative, and in many cases, may be based on stereotypes (the cognitive component) about the specific group.	A stereotype is a cluster of ideas regarding the characteristics of a specific group.
(ii)	Prejudice may also get translated into discrimination, the behavioural component, when people behave in a less positive way towards a particular target group compared to another group which they favour.	Stereotypes consist of undesirable characteristics about the target group, and they lead to negative attitudes or prejudices towards members of specific groups. Thus, prejudice may be based on stereotypes.

11. State the strategies for overcoming prejudice.

Ans. The first step in handling prejudice is to know about its causes or sources. Thus, the strategies for handling prejudice would be effective if they aim at

- Minimising opportunities for learning prejudices.
- Changing such attitudes.
- De-emphasising a narrow social identity based on the ingroup.
- Discouraging the tendency towards self-fulfilling prophecy among the victims of prejudice.

These goals can be accomplished through

- Education and information dissemination, for correcting stereotypes related to specific target groups, and tackling the problem of a strong ingroup bias.
- Increasing intergroup contact allows for direct communication, removal of mistrust between the groups, and even discovery of positive qualities in the outgroup. These strategies are successful only if
  (a) The two groups meet in a cooperative rather than competitive context.
  (b) Close interactions between the groups helps them to know each other better.
  (c) The two groups are not different in power or status.
- Highlighting individual identity rather than group identity, which weaken the importance of group (both ingroup and outgroup) as a basis of evaluating the other person.

• Long Answer (LA) Type Questions

1. Are attitudes learnt? Explain how.　　　(NCERT)

Or Explain the conditions which lead to the learning of attitudes.　　　(**Delhi 2016**)

Or Explain the process involved in the learning of attitudes　　　(**CBSE Sample Paper 2020**)

Ans. Yes, attitudes are learnt. It can be explained as follows

Learning Attitudes by Association You might have seen that students often develop a liking for a particular subject because of the positive qualities in that teacher. These positive qualities get linked to the subject that she/he teaches and ultimately get expressed in the form of liking for the subject.

Learning Attitudes by Being Rewarded or Punished If an individual is praised for showing a particular attitude, chances are high that she/he will develop that attitude further.

Learning Attitudes through Modelling (observing others) We learn attitudes by observing others being rewarded or punished for expressing thoughts, or showing behaviour of a particular kind towards the attitude object.

Learning Attitudes through Group or Cultural Norms We learn attitudes through the norms of our group or culture. Norms are unwritten rules about behaviour that everyone is supposed to show under specific circumstances. Over time, these norms may become part of our social cognition in the form of attitudes.

Learning through Exposure to Information Many attitudes are learned in a social context, but not necessarily in the physical presence of others. Today, with the huge amount of information that is being provided through various media, both positive and negative attitudes are being formed. By reading the biographies of self-actualised persons, an individual may develop a positive attitude towards hard work and other aspects as the means of achieving success in life.

2. A driver in the army went through a certain experience that transformed his life. On one mission, he narrowly escaped death although all his companions got killed. Wondering about the purpose of his own life, he gave up his job in the army, returned to his native village in Maharashtra, and worked actively as a community leader.

Identify the factor that affected the attitude formation in army driver. Also, give a brief about other factors that shapes the attitude formation.

Ans. In the given case study, army driver transformed his life through a purely personal experience when he narrowly escaped death. This individual evolved a strong positive attitude towards community upliftment and evolved as a community leader. As a community leader, his efforts completely changed the face of his village. Many attitudes are formed, not in the family environment or through reference groups, but through direct personal experiences which bring about a drastic change in our attitude towards people and our own life as it happened in this case.

Other factors that shape the attitude formation are as follows

- **Family and School Environment** In the early years of life, parents and other family members play a significant role in shaping attitude formation. Later, the school environment becomes an important background for attitude formation.
  Learning of attitudes within the family and school usually takes place by association, through rewards and punishments, and through modelling.
- **Reference Groups** Reference groups indicate to an individual the norms regarding acceptable behaviour and ways of thinking. Thus, they reflect learning of attitudes through group or cultural norms.
- **Media-Related Influences** Technological advances in recent times have made audio-visual media and the Internet very powerful sources of information that lead to attitude formation and change.

3. What are the factors that influence the formation of an attitude?　　　(**Delhi 2017**)

Ans. The following factors influence the learning of attitudes

1. **Family and School Environment** It plays a significant role in shaping attitude formation. Learning of attitudes within the family and school usually takes place by association, through rewards and punishments and through modelling.

2. **Reference Groups** It indicates to an individual the norms regarding acceptable behaviour and ways of thinking. Thus, they reflect learning of attitudes through group or cultural norms. Attitudes towards various topics, such as political, religious and social groups, occupations, national and other issues are often developed through reference groups.

3. **Personal Experiences** Many attitudes are formed through direct personal experiences which bring about a drastic change in our attitude towards people and our own life.

4. **Media-related Influences** Technological advances in recent times have made audio-visual media and the Internet very powerful sources of information that lead to attitude formation and change. In addition, school level textbooks also influence attitude formation. These sources first strengthen the cognitive and affective components of attitudes and gradually may affect the behavioural component.

4. Radhika was fond of junk food and ate it too often. However, she always felt guilty as she knew junk food was harmful for her health and wanted to give it up. Explain the process that will lead to change in her attitude. **(CBSE Sample Paper 2020)**

Ans. The process that will lead to change in her attitude is cognitive dissonance. The concept of cognitive dissonance was proposed by Leon Festinger. It emphasises the cognitive component. Here the basic idea is that the cognitive components of an attitude must be 'consonant' (opposite of 'dissonant'), i.e., they should be logically in line with each other. If an individual finds that two cognitions in an attitude are dissonant, then one of them will be changed in the direction of consonance. For example, think about the following ideas.

Cognition I : Junk foods are harmful for health. It can lead to obesity, increase sugar level and weight gain.

Cognition II : I eat Junk food.

Holding these two ideas or cognitions will make any individual feel that something is 'out of tune', or dissonant, in the attitude towards junk food. Therefore, one of these ideas will have to be changed, so that consonance can be attained. In the example given above, in order to remove or reduce the dissonance, I will stop eating junk food (change Cognition II). This would be the healthy, logical and sensible way of reducing dissonance.

5. State the factors that influence attitude change.
(All India 2017)

Ans. The major factors that influence attitude change are as follows

(i) **Characteristics of the Existing Attitude** All four features (valence, extremeness, simplicity and centrality) of attitudes determine attitude change. In general, positive attitudes are easier to change than negative attitudes. Simple attitudes are easier to change than multiple attitudes. An attitude change may be congruent (favourable) or incongruent (not favourable).

(ii) **Source Characteristics** Source credibility and attractiveness are two features that affect attitude change. Attitudes are more likely to change when the message comes from a highly credible source rather than from a low-credible source.

(iii) **Message Characteristics** The message is the information that is presented in order to bring about an attitude change. Attitudes will change when the amount of information that is given about the topic is just enough, neither too much nor too little.

The message contains emotional appeal, motives and moods of it also play significant role. Face-to-face transmission of the message is usually more effective than indirect transmission i.e. through letters and pamphlets or even through mass media.

(iv) **Target Characteristics** Qualities of the target, such as persuasibility, strong prejudices, self-esteem and intelligence influence the likelihood and extent of attitude change.

People who have a more open and flexible personality, change more easily. People with strong preconceptions are less prone or inclined to any attitude change.

More intelligent people may change their attitudes less easily than those with lower intelligence.

6. Is behaviour always a reflection of one's attitude? Explain with a relevant example.

Ans. An individual's attitudes may not always be exhibited through behaviour. One's actual behaviour may be contrary to one's attitude towards a particular topic. Attitudes may not always predict actual pattern of one's behaviour. Sometimes, it is behaviour that decides the attitude.

Psychologists have found that there would be consistency between attitudes and behaviour when

- The attitude is strong, and occupies a central place in the attitude system.
- The person is aware of her/his attitude.
- There is very little or no external pressure for the person to behave in a particular way.
- The person's behaviour is not being watched or evaluated by others.
- The person thinks that the behaviour would have a positive consequence and therefore, intends to engage in that behaviour.

In the days when Americans were said to be prejudiced against the Chinese, Richard La Piere, an American social psychologist, conducted the following study. He asked a Chinese couple to travel across the United States, and stay in different hotels. Only once during these occasions they were refused service by one of the hotels. Sometime later, La Piere sent out questionnaires to managers of hotels and tourist homes in the same areas where the Chinese couple had travelled, asking them if they would give accommodation to Chinese guests. A very large percentage said that they would not do so.

This response showed a negative attitude towards the Chinese, which was inconsistent with the positive behaviour that was actually shown towards the travelling Chinese couple. Thus, attitudes may not always predict actual pattern of one's behaviour.

• Case Based Questions

1. An attitude is a state of the mind, a set of views or thoughts, regarding some topics (called the 'attitude object'), which have an evaluative feature (positive, negative or neutral quality). It is accompanied by an emotional component and a tendency to act in a particular way with regard to the attitude object. If our views are not merely thoughts, but also have emotional and action components, then these views are the examples of attitudes.

The thought component is referred to as the cognitive aspect, the emotional component is known as the affective aspect and the tendency to act is called the behavioural (or cognitive) aspect. These three aspects have been referred to as the A-B-C components i.e. Affective-Behavioural and Cognitive components of attitude.

(i) What is the difference between attitude, beliefs and values?

Ans. Values are attitudes or beliefs that contain a 'should' or 'ought to' aspect, such as moral or ethical values. Attitudes have to be distinguished from two other closely related concepts, namely beliefs and values.

Beliefs refer to the cognitive component of attitudes and form the ground on which attitudes stand, such as belief in God or belief in democracy as a political ideology.

(ii) What are the various features of attitude? Explain in detail.

Ans. Four significant features of attitudes are as follows

1. **Valence (Positivity or Negativity)** The valence of an attitude tells us whether an attitude is positive or negative towards the attitude object.

2. **Extremeness** The extremeness of an attitude indicates how positive or negative an attitude is.

3. **Simplicity or Complexity (Multiplicity)** This feature refers to how many attitudes are there within a broader attitude.

4. **Centrality** An attitude with greater centrality would influence the other attitudes in the system much more than non-central (or peripheral) attitudes.

(iii) Explain the factors that influence attitude formation.

Ans. The following factors influence the learning of attitudes

1. **Family and School Environment** Learning of attitudes within the family and school usually takes place by association, through rewards and punishments and through modelling.

2. **Reference Groups** It indicates to an individual the norms regarding acceptable behaviour and ways of thinking.

3. **Personal Experiences** Many attitudes are formed through direct personal experiences.

4. **Media-related Influences** Technological advances in recent times have made audio-visual media and the Internet very powerful sources of information that lead to attitude formation and change.

2. In the days when Americans were said to be prejudiced against the Chinese, Richard LaPiere, an American social psychologist, conducted the following study. He asked a Chinese couple to travel across the United States, and stay in different hotels. Only once during these occasions they were refused service by one of the hotels. Sometime later, LaPiere sent out questionnaires to managers of hotels and tourist homes in the same areas where the Chinese couple had travelled, asking them if they would give accommodation to Chinese guests. A very large percentage said that they would not do so. This response showed a negative attitude towards the Chinese, which was inconsistent with the positive behaviour that was actually shown towards the travelling Chinese couple. Thus, attitudes may not always predict actual pattern of one's behaviour.

(i) Explain the sources of prejudices.

Ans. Social psychologists have shown that prejudice has the following sources

Learning Like other attitudes, prejudices can also be learned through association, reward and punishment, etc.

A Strong Social Identity and Ingroup Bias Individuals who have a strong sense of social identity and have a very positive attitude towards their own group boost this attitude by holding negative attitudes towards other groups. These are shown as prejudices.

Scapegoating This is a phenomenon by which the majority group places the blame on a minority outgroup for its own social, economic or political problems.

Kernel of Truth Concept Sometimes people may continue to hold stereotypes because they think that there must be some truth or 'kernel of truth' is what everyone says about the other group.

(ii) Discuss the goals of handling prejudices.

Ans. These goals can be accomplished through

- Education and information dissemination, for correcting stereotypes related to specific target groups and tackling the problem of a strong ingroup bias.

- Increasing intergroup contact allows for direct communication, removal of mistrust between the groups and even discovery of positive qualities in the outgroup.

(iii) Give strategies for handling prejudices.

Ans. The strategies for handling prejudice would be effective if they aim at

- Minimising opportunities for learning prejudices.
- Changing prejudice attitudes.
- De-emphasising a narrow social identity based on the ingroup.
- Discouraging the tendency towards self-fulfilling prophecy among the victims of prejudice.

3. Sunaina had a habit of using foul language. She had no friends and could not sustain a single job due to her bad language. After she got married her husband Started putting great effort into changing her attitude. He always kept reminding her to calm down the moment she got agitated and used foul language. He also made a punishment jar at home in which anyone who spoke in a bad way would put 1₹. At the end of the month he used the collected money to buy something for the house. After some time, Sunaina's language improved considerably. Her temper issues also got in control. Now the jar remained empty.

(i) Can you explain P-O-X based on Sunaina's case?

Ans. The P-O-X triangle represents the relationships between three aspects or components of the attitude.

- P is the person whose attitude is being studied.
- O is another person.
- X is the topic towards which the attitude is being studied (attitude object).

In this case, P is Sunaina, O is her husband and X is attitude of speaking foul language.

(ii) Name the factors which influenced change in Sunaina's attitude.

Ans. Following are the major factors that influence attitude change

Characteristics of the Existing Attitude All four features (valence, extremeness, simplicity and centrality) of attitudes determine attitude change.

Source Characteristics: Source credibility and attractiveness are two features that affect attitude change.

Message Characteristics The message is the information that is presented in order to bring about an attitude change.

Target Characteristics Qualities of the target, such as persuasibility, strong prejudices, self-esteem and intelligence influence the likelihood and extent of attitude change.

(iii) Throw some light on the relationship between Sunaina's attitude and behaviour.

Ans. An individual's attitude may not always be exhibited through behaviour. One's actual behaviour may be contrary to one's attitude towards a particular topic. Attitudes may not always predict the actual pattern of one's behaviour. Sometimes, it is behaviour that decides the attitude.

Chapter Test

Multiple Choice Questions

1. The tendency to act is known as
   (a) The cognitive aspect   (b) The behavioural aspect   (c) The affective aspect   (d) None of these

2. Which is a significant feature of attitudes?
   (a) Valence   (b) Extremeness   (c) Simplicity   (d) All of these

3. Which of the following indicates how positive or negative an attitude is?
   (a) Centrality   (b) Valence   (c) Extremeness   (d) All of these

4. Consider the following statements:

Case I People, who have a more open and flexible personality, change more easily.

Case II People with strong prejudices are less prone to any attitude change than those who do not hold strong prejudices.

On the basis of two cases, which factor/s is more likely to contribute or influence the likelihood and extent of attitude change?
   (a) Persuasibility   (b) Strong prejudices   (c) Self-esteem and intelligence   (d) All of these

5. Who suggested that stable factors are factors that do not change with time?
   (a) Mohsin   (b) Triplett   (c) Heider   (d) Wiener

Short Answer (SA) Type Questions

6. Define the various types of attitude.

7. What are the causes of emergence of prejudice?

8. State the sources of prejudice.

9. Explain P-O-X triangle in attitude change.

10. An advertisement for cooking food in a pressure cooker points out that this saves fuel such as cooking gas (LPG) and is economical. Another advertisement says that pressure-cooking preserves nutrition, and that if one cares for the family, nutrition would be a major concern. Compare the two advertisements and identify the message characteristics in both. Do also differentiate in between the two advertisements.

Long Answer (LA) Type Questions

11. What are the important process of attitude change?

12. Discuss the characteristics of prejudice.

13. Preeti reads in the newspapers that a particular soft drink that she enjoys is extremely harmful. But Preeti sees that her favourite sportsperson has been advertising the same soft drink. She has identified herself with the sportsperson, and would like to imitate her/him. How do you think Preeti will able to change her habit? Identify the process of attitude change in this case? Give all the steps involved in attitude change of Preeti.

Answers

1. (a)   *2.* (b)   *3.* (d)   *4.* (b)   *5.* (d)

CHAPTER 04

Social Influence and Group Processes

In this Chapter...

- Introduction
- Nature and Formation of Groups
- Types of Groups
- Influence of Group on Individual Behaviour
- Social Loafing
- Group Polarisation

Introduction

In this chapter we shall try to understand about Groups and their influence on our behaviour.

Similarly, we would try to understand about group conflicts and strategies to resolve conflicts for harmonious and united society.

Nature and Formation of Groups

A group may be defined as an organised system of two or more interdependent individuals, who have common motives and norms to regulate the behaviour of its members.

A group not only provides us the needed support and comfort but also facilitates our growth and development as an individual. Our lives are influenced by the nature of group membership we have. It is very important to be a part of group which influences us positively and helps us in becoming good citizens. It is not only that others influence us, but we as individuals are also capable of changing others and the society.

Characteristics of a Group

Groups have the following salient characteristics

- It is a social unit consisting of two or more individuals who perceive themselves as belonging to the group. This characteristic of the group helps in distinguishing one group from the other and gives the group its unique identity.
- It is a collection of individuals who have common motives and goals. A group functions to achieve a desired goal or to keep away from certain threats faced by the group.
- It is a collection of individuals who are interdependent, i.e. what one is doing may have consequences for others. For example, if a fielder in a cricket team drops an important catch during the match, it will have consequence for the entire team.
- Individuals who are trying to satisfy a need through their joint association also influence each other.
- It is a gathering of individuals who interact with one another either directly or indirectly.
- It is a collection of individuals whose interactions are structured by a set of roles and norms. This means that the group members perform the same functions every time the group meets. Norm specify the behaviours expected from the group members.

Groups can be differentiated from other collections of people. These are

- **Crowd** A crowd is a collection of people who may be present at a place/situation by chance. Behaviour of people in crowds is irrational and there is no interdependence among members. For example, if you are going on the road and an accident takes place, a large number of people come there. This is an elaborate example of crowd. There is no feeling of belongingness and interdependence among members of a crowd.

- **Teams** These are special kinds of groups. Members of teams often have complementary skills and are committed to a common goal or purpose. Members are mutually accountable for their activities. In teams, there is a positive synergy (teamwork) attained through the coordinated efforts of the members.

- **Audience** It is a collection of people who have assembled for a special purpose, e.g. to watch a cricket match or a movie. Generally, audiences are passive but sometimes they go into a frenzy and become mobs. Mob behaviour is characterised by homogeneity of thought and behaviour as well as impulsivity.

Differences between Groups and Teams

- In groups, performance is dependent on contributions of individual members. In teams, both individual contributions and teamwork matter.
- In groups, the leader or whoever is leading the group holds responsibility for the work. However in teams, although there is a leader, members hold themselves responsible.

Reasons of Joining Groups

People join groups because these groups satisfy a range of needs. Following are reasons to join groups

- **Security** Groups reduce the feeling of insecurity when we are alone. Being with people gives a sense of comfort and protection. As a result, people feel stronger and are less vulnerable to threats.

- **Status** When we are members of a group that is perceived to be important by others, we feel recognised and experience a sense of power.

  For example, when a school wins an inter-institutional debate competition, students feel proud and think that they are better than others.

- **Self-esteem** Groups provide feelings of self-worth and establish a positive social identity. Being a member of prestigious groups enhances one's self-concept.

- **Satisfaction of One's Psychological and Social Needs** Groups satisfy one's social and psychological needs such

as sense of belongingness, giving and receiving attention, love and power through a group.

- **Goal Achievement** Groups help in achieving such goals which cannot be attained individually. There is power in the majority.

- **Provide Knowledge and Information** Group membership provides knowledge and information and thus broadens our view. As individuals, we may not have all the required information.

Group Formation

Groups are formed by making contacts through or interactions between people. This interaction is facilitated by the following conditions

Proximity Repeated interactions with the same set of individuals give us a chance to know them and their interests and attitudes. Common interests, attitudes and background are important determinants of our liking for our group members.

Similarity Being exposed to someone over a period of time makes us assess our similarities and paves the way for formation of groups. We like people who are similar because people prefer consistency and like relationships that are consistent. When two people are similar, there is consistency and they start liking each other.

For example, I like playing football and one of my batch mate also like playing football. There is a high chances that we may become friends as our interests are same.

Common Motives and Goals When people have common motives or goals, they get together and form a group which may facilitate their goal attainment.

For example, I want to teach children in a slum area who are unable to go to school. I can form a group with like minded friends and start teaching these children. In this way I can achieve my goal with the help of others.

Stages of Group Formation

Tuckman suggested that groups pass through five developmental sequences. These are as follows

(i) **Forming** When group members meet for the first time, a kind of uncertainty is created for achieving group goals. People try to know each other and assess whether they will fit in or not. There is excitement as well as apprehensions. This stage is called the forming stage.

(ii) **Storming** After forming stage, there is a stage of intragroup conflict which is referred to as storming. In this stage, there is conflict among members about the target, process, performance and control of resources. When this stage is complete, **hierarchy of leadership** in the group develops.

(*iii*) **Norming** The storming stage is followed by another stage known as norming. Group members by this time develop norms related to group behaviour. This leads to development of a **positive group identity**.

(*iv*) **Performing** By this stage the structure of the group has evolved and is accepted by group members. The group moves towards achieving the group goal. For some groups, this may be the last stage of group development.

(*v*) **Adjourning** In this stage, once the function is over, the group may be disbanded. However, all groups do not always proceed from one stage to the next in the same manner.

Group Structure

During the process of group formation, groups also develop a structure as members interact. Over the time, this interaction shows regularities in distribution of task to be performed, responsibilities assigned to members and the prestige or relative status of members.

Four important elements of group structure are as follows

(*i*) **Roles** These are socially defined expectations that individuals in a given situation are expected to fulfil. Roles refer to the typical behaviour that depicts a person in a given social context.

Every individual has to play some role. As a daughter or son she/he has to respect elders, listen to them and be responsible towards their studies. There are certain role expectations, i.e. behaviour expected of someone in a particular role.

(*ii*) **Norms** These are expected standards of behaviour and beliefs established, agreed upon and enforced by group members. For example, in every family there are norms that guide the behaviour of family members which represent their views of the world.

(*iii*) **Status** It refers to the relative social position given to group members by others. This relative position or status may be either **ascribed** (given may be because of one's seniority) or **achieved** (the person has achieved status because of expertise or hard work).

For example, the caption of a cricket team has a higher status compared to other members inspite of all players are equally important for the team's success.

(*iv*) **Cohesiveness** It refers to togetherness, binding or mutual attraction among group members. As the group becomes more cohesive, group members start to think, feel and act as a social unit, and less like isolated individuals. Members of a highly cohesive group have more desire to remain in the group in comparison to those who belong to low cohesive groups.

Cohesiveness refer to the team spirit or 'we feeling' a sense of belongingness to the group. Psychologists suggest groupthink which is a consequence of extreme cohesiveness.

Groupthink

Irving Janis discovered a process known as **groupthink** in which a group allows its concerns for unanimity. They override the motivation to realistically appraise courses of action. It results in the tendency of decision makers to make irrational and uncritical decisions.

Groupthink suggests the appearance of consensus or unanimous agreement within a group. All members of a group agree upon a particular decision of the group. No one express dissenting (expressing) opinion as it can destroy the cohesion of the group.

There are also some ways to prevent groupthink. These are as follows

- Encouraging and rewarding critical thinking.
- Encouraging groups to present alternative courses of action.
- Inviting outside experts to evaluate the group's decisions.
- Encouraging members to seek feedback from trusted others.

Types of Groups

Groups may be different in many respects. Some have a large number of members e.g. a country, some are small e.g. a family, some are short-lived e.g. a committee, some remain together for many years e.g. religious groups, some are highly organised e.g. army, police, etc., and others are informally organised e.g. spectators of a match.

Major types of groups are discussed below

Primary and Secondary Groups

Primary groups are pre-existing formations, which are usually given to the individual. Thus, **family, caste** and **religion** are primary groups. In a primary group, there is a face-to-face interaction, members have close physical proximity and they share warm emotional bonds.

Primary groups are central to individual's functioning and have a very major role in developing values and ideals of the individual during the early stages of development. In the primary group, boundaries are less permeable, i.e. members do not have the option to choose its membership.

Secondary groups are those which the individual joins by choice. Membership of a political party is an example of a secondary group. Secondary groups are those where relationships among members are more impersonal, indirect and less frequent. In secondary groups, it is easy to leave and join another group.

Formal and Informal Groups

The formation of formal groups is based on some specific rules or laws and members have definite roles. There are a set of norms which help in establishing order. A **university** is an example of a formal group.

The functions of a formal group are explicitly (clearly) stated in the case of an office organisation. The formation of informal groups is not based on rules or laws and there is close relationship among members.

Ingroup and Outgroup

The term ingroup refers to one's own group and outgroup refers to another group. For ingroup members, we use the word 'we' while for outgroup members, the word 'they' is used. By using the words we and they, one is categorising people as similar or different.

People in the ingroup are generally similar, seen favourably and have desirable traits. Members of the outgroup are viewed differently and are often perceived negatively in comparison to the ingroup members.

Perceptions of ingroup and outgroup affect our social lives. In some cultures, plurality is celebrated as in India. We have a unique composite culture which is reflected not only in the lives we live, but also in our art, architecture and music.

Influence of Group on Individual Behaviour

Groups are powerful, as they are able to influence the behaviour of individuals. Two situations to understand the nature and impact of group influence are as follows

(i) An individual performing an activity alone in the presence of others (social facilitation).

(ii) An individual performing an activity along with the others as part of a larger group (social loafing).

Social Loafing

Social loafing is a reduction in individual effort when working in a group. Such situations give opportunities to group members to relax and become a free rider.

This phenomenon has been demonstrated in many experiments by **Latane** and his associates. They asked group of male students to clap or cheer as loudly as possible because they wanted to know how much noise people make in social settings. The result revealed that although the total amount of noise rose up, the amount of noise produced by each participant dropped.

Some reasons for the occurring of social loafing are as follows

- Group members feel less responsible for the overall task being performed and therefore exert less effort.
- Motivation of members decreases because they realise that their contributions will not be evaluated on individual basis.
- The performance of the group is not to be compared with other groups.
- There is an improper coordination (or no coordination) among members.
- Belonging to the same group is not important for members. It is only an aggregate of individuals.

Some measures to reduce social loafing are as follows

- Making the efforts of each person identifiable.
- Increasing the pressure to work hard (making group members committed to successful task performance).
- Increasing the apparent importance or value of a task.
- Making people feel that their individual contribution is important.
- Strengthening group cohesiveness which increases the motivation for successful group outcome.

Group Polarisation

Group polarisation focuses on **how groups usually make decisions** that are more extreme than the original thoughts and views of the individual team members. It refers to the tendency of a group to make decisions that are more extreme than the initial inclination of its members. For example, suppose you favour **capital punishment**[1] for heinous crimes and you were interacting this issue with like-minded people. After this interaction, your views may become stronger.

This firm conviction is because of the following three reasons

(i) In the company of like-minded people, you are likely to hear newer arguments favouring your viewpoints.

(ii) When you find others also favouring capital punishment, you feel that this view is validated by the public. This is a type of **bandwagon effect**[2].

(iii) When you find people having similar views, you are likely to perceive them as ingroup. You start identifying with the group, begin showing conformity and as a consequence your views become strengthened.

---

1 **Capital Punishment** The legally authorised killing of someone as punishment.
2 **Bandwagon Effect** It is a Phychological phenomenon in which people do something primarily because other people are doing it.

Chapter Practice

Objective Questions

• Multiple Choice Questions

1. A collection of people who may be present at a place/situation by chance is known as ________.
(a) crowd
(b) teams
(c) audience
(d) None of these

Ans. (a) A crowd is a collection of people who may be present at a place/situation by chance.

2. In a society, people have assembled for a special purpose i.e., to watch a cricket match in between India and Pakistan. In this case, assembly of people can be called as ________ .
(a) Crowd
(b) Team
(c) Audience
(d) Association

Ans. (c) In this case, assembly of people can be called as Audience.

3. Which among the following is not a reason for joining a group?
(a) Security
(b) Status
(c) Self-esteem
(d) All of these

Ans. (d) Security, status and self-esteem are the reasons for forming a group.

4. Aneesh has friends from housing society and school where he lives in and studies. In this case, Aneesh was able to made friends because of ________ .
(a) Similarity
(b) Social loafing
(c) Obedience
(d) Proximity

Ans. (d) In this case, Aneesh was able to made friends because of Proximity.

5. Which of the following is not a characteristic of a group?
(a) It is a social unit consisting of two or more individuals who perceive themselves as belonging to the group.
(b) It is a collection of individuals who have common motives and goals.
(c) It is a collection of individuals who are not interdependent.
(d) Individuals who are trying to satisfy a need through their joint association also influence each other.

Ans. (c) The given option (c) i.e. It is a collection of individuals who are not interdependent is not a characteristic of a group.

6. Who had suggested the five development sequences of group formation?
(a) Ivan Pavlov
(b) Tuckman
(c) Kelman
(d) B.F. Skinner

Ans. (b) Tuckman had suggested the five developmental sequences of group formation.

7. Piyush was part of a group where everyone was a non-drinker. In fact nobody liked drinking at all. However, one member of the group, Vijay, started drinking. Whenever the group met, Vijay helped himself with a few drinks. This was not very well appreciated by the rest of the members of the group and hence, Vijay was soon moved out of the group. Which element of the group did Vijay did not comply?
(a) Norm
(b) Rule
(c) Culture
(d) Pact

Ans. (a) Vijay did not comply with the norm element of Group. As Norms is the expected behaviour of shared rules varying from different cultures in the world.

8. ________ refers to the relative social position given to group members by others.
(a) Status
(b) Norms
(c) Cohesiveness
(d) Roles

Ans. (a) Status refers to the relative social position given to group members by others.

9. Feeling of togetherness that keep a group intact is
(a) Norms
(b) Role
(c) Status
(d) Cohesiveness

Ans. (d) Feeling of togetherness that keep a group intact is cohesiveness.

10. Membership of a club is an example of ________ .
(a) Primary group
(b) Secondary group
(c) Outgroup
(d) Large group

Ans. (b) Membership of a club is an example of secondary group.

11. Lata left the tap on by mistake one morning. Lots of people in her colony saw the tap running but nobody closed it thinking that someone else would do it as it is everyone's responsibility to save water. This type of attitude is known as ________ .
(a) Obedience   (b) Social loafing
(c) Norm   (d) Group polarisation

Ans. (b) This type of attitude is known as social loafing. Social loafing is a reduction in individual effort when working on a collective task, i.e. one in which outputs are combined with those of other group members.

12. Which of the following statements are true about social loafing?
1. Group members feel responsible for the overall task being performed and therefore exert less effort.
2. Motivation of members decreases because they realise that their contributions will not be evaluated on individual basis.
3. The performance of the group is not to be compared with other groups.
4. There is an improper coordination (or no coordination) among members.

Choose the correct option
(a) 1,2,3   (b) 2,3,4
(c) 4,1,2   (d) 1,3

Ans. (b) Statements 2, 3 and 4 are true about social loafing but statement 1 is not true as group members feel less responsible for the overall task being performed and therefore exert less effort in social loafing.

13. After a long discussion, the initial position of the group became much stronger. This demonstrating the effect of ________ .
(a) Group polarisation   (b) Group conformity
(c) Group think   (d) Group cohesiveness

Ans. (a) This demonstrating the effect of Group polarisation.

14. Rahul has always been against dowry but one day in office discussion when majority was supporting dowry then he also went with the flow and started speaking in favour of the rotten norm of the society. This effect is more commonly known as
(a) Compliance   (b) Personality
(c) Conformity   (d) Bandwagon effect

Ans. (d) This effect given is more commonly known as Bandwagon effect.

15. Which of the following statements are true about team?
(a) Teams are special kind of groups.
(b) In teams, members are mutually accountable for their activities.
(c) Members of teams often have complementary skills.
(d) In team, the leader is heading the group holds responsibility for the work.

Ans. (a) Statements 1, 2 and 3 are true about team but statement 4 is not true as it is a group wherein leader is heading the group holds responsibility for the work.

• Assertion-Reasoning MCQs

Direction (Q. Nos. 1-4) *Each of these questions contains two statements, Assertion (A) and Reason (R). Each of these question also has four alternative choices, any one of which is the correct answer. You have to select one of the codes (a), (b), (c) and (d) given below.*
(a) Both A and R are true and R is the correct explanation of A
(b) Both A and R are true, but R is not the correct explanation of A
(c) A is true, but R is false
(d) A is false, but R is true

1. Assertion (A) Roles are socially defined expectations that individuals in a given situation are expected to fulfil.

Reason (R) Status refers to the relative social position given to group members by others.

Ans. (b) Both A and R are true, but R is not the correct explanation of A. Roles are socially defined expectations that individuals in a given situation are expected to fulfil. Roles refer to the typical behaviour that depicts a person in a given social context.
Status refers to the relative social position given to group members by others. Hence, R does not explain A.

2. Assertion (A) Members of a highly cohesive group have more desire to remain in the group in comparison to those who belong to low cohesive groups.

Reason (R) As the group becomes more cohesive, group members start to think, feel and act as a social unit, and less like isolated individuals.

Ans. (a) Both A and R are true and R is the correct explanation of A. Cohesiveness refers to togetherness, as the group becomes more cohesive, the group members start feeling and act as a social unit. Hence, members of cohesive group are more likely to remain in the group in comparison to those who belong to low cohesive groups.

3. Assertion (A) The formation of formal groups is based on some specific rules or laws and members have definite roles.

Reason (R) There are a set of norms which help in establishing order.

Ans. (a) Both A and R are true and R is the correct explanation of A. Formation of formal groups is based on some specific rules or laws which is establishing order to the group and a code of conduct to the organisation.

4. Assertion (A) Social loafing is a reduction in individual effort when working on a collective task.

Reason (R) It has been found that individual work is less hard in a group.

Ans. (a) Both A and R are true and R is the correct explanation of A. In social loafing an individual efforts reduces when working in a collective task.

• Case Based MCQs

1. Atul was a simple middle class person with no issues with anyone. One day he and his friends went to a restaurant for dinner. They had a good time. Later when the bill came, Atul, an extra charge of 40 Rs. had been added on the bill.

Atul and his friends called out to the waiter for an explanation. The waiter agreed to his fault and said sorry. However, Atul and his friends pushed the topic. One of his friends took out the phone and made a video of the restaurant, defaming it unnecessarily. Later, all the friends decided to make the video go viral on social media. Due to the defamation caused by the video, the hotel manager fired the poor waiter who was the sole earning member of the family. Later when Atul learnt about this, he felt very guilty that he was involved in the unnecessary action of viraling the video. He feels that had he been alone he would not have taken such an extreme decision for just ₹ 40.

(i) Atul took an extreme decision under the influence of his friends. What is such type of behaviour called?
(a) Social loafing
(b) Group polarisation
(c) Conformity
(d) Obedience

Ans. (b) Such type of Behaviour is called Group polarisation. It focuses on how groups usually make decisions that are more extreme than the original thoughts and views of the individual team members.

(ii) How would you rate the decision of Atul about video viraling?
(a) Very extreme
(b) Too mild
(c) Not too harsh
(d) It was not his fault that the waiter got fired

Ans. (a) Atul decided to defame a restaurant only for ₹ 40. Without going through his thoughts. This decision was very extreme and impulsive.

(iii) Which of the following is not a form of social influence?
(a) Compliance
(b) Identification
(c) Internalisation
(d) Externalisation

Ans. (d) Externalisation is not a form of social influence. The three forms of social influence are compliance, identification and internalisation.

(iv) Which of the following is the definition of Bandwagon effect?
(a) When nobody supports your view.
(b) When a view is supported by a few people and so you think that it is right.
(c) When you understand that few people supporting an idea does not make it a right idea.
(d) When there is multiple ideas over a topic.

Ans. (b) When a view is supported by a few people and so you think that it is right is the definition of bandwagon effect.

The bandwagon effect is a psychological phenomenon in which people do something primarily because other people are doing it, regardless of their own beliefs .

(v) What happens when someone has the same views as ours?
(a) We see that person as an in group
(b) We see that person as someone not belong to the group
(c) We see that person as our best friend
(d) None of the above

Ans. (a) When someone has the same views as ours, we often see that person as a part of our group.

(vi) **Assertion (A)** Group polarisation focuses on how groups usually make decisions that are more extreme than the original thoughts and views of the individual team members.

Reason (R) In the company of like-minded people, you are likely to hear newer arguments favouring your viewpoints.

Choose the correct option
(a) Both A and R are true and R is the correct explanation of A
(b) Both A and R are true, but R is not the a correct explanation of A
(c) A is true, but R is false
(d) R is true, but A is false

Ans. (a) Both A and R are true, R is the correct explanation for A. Group polarisation focuses usually make decisions that are more extreme in company of like-minded people. You are likely to hear newer arguments.

Subjective Questions

• Short Answer (SA) Type Questions

1. Describe the characteristics of the group.

Ans. The characteristics of the group are as follows

- It is a social unit consisting of two or more individuals who perceive themselves as belonging to the group. This characteristic of the group helps in distinguishing one group from the other and gives the group its unique identity.
- It is a collection of individuals who have common motives and goals. Groups function either working towards a given goal or away from certain threats facing the group.
- It is a collection of individuals who are interdependent, i.e. what one is doing may have consequences for others.
- Individuals who are trying to satisfy a need through their joint association also influence each other.
- It is a gathering of individuals who interact with one another either directly or indirectly.
- It is a collection of individuals whose interactions are structured by a set of roles and norms.

2. Explain how crowd is different from the groups.

Ans. A group is an organised system of two or more individuals who are interacting and interdependent. The members of a group have common motives, have a set of role relationships among its members. The group has norms that regulate the behaviour of its members.

On the other hand, a crowd is also a collection of people who may be present at a place/situation by chance. For example, person is going on the road and an accident takes place. Soon a large number of people tend to collect. There is neither any structure nor feeling of belongingness in a crowd. Behaviour of people in crowds is irrational and there is no interdependence among members. There is no norms that regulate the behaviour of the crowd.

3. Explain the term audience and mob.

Ans. **Audience** is a collection of people participating in different ways for a special purpose, may be to watch a cricket match or a movie. Audiences are generally passive but sometimes they go into a frenzy and become mobs.

Mob is an unruly and often violent group of people , especially one engaged in a riot or other lawless violence. In mob there is a definite sense of purpose.
There is polarisation in attention and actions of persons are in a common direction. Mob behaviour is characterised by homogeneity of thought and behaviour as well as impulsivity.

4. Cricket team in Ranjan's locality is very famous. Ranjan and his group of friends are active members in this team. What are the main difference between their group and team?

Ans. The main differences between group of Ranjan and his friends and their cricket team are as follows

Group	Team
In Ranjan and his friends' group, performance is dependent on contributions of individual members.	In cricket team both individual contributions and teamwork matter.
In group, Ranjan is the leader who is leading the group and taking the responsibility for the work of the group.	In cricket team, although there is a captain (leader), members hold themselves responsible for the performance of the team.
Group have a small degree of interdependence.	Team has a higher degree of interdependence.

5. In school Pooja joins the dance group. What are the reasons that led her to join this group?

Ans Pooja joins the dance group for the following reasons

(i) **Security** Being with other friends gives a sense of comfort and protection to Pooja.

(ii) **Status** Being a member of the dance group, Pooja fell recognised and experience a sense of power. When their school wins in an Inter-School Dance Competition, Pooja feels proud and thinks that she is better than others.

(iii) **Self-esteem** This group enhances Pooja's self concept or self-worth and establish a positive social identity.

(iv) **Satisfaction of One's Psychological and Social Needs** Dance group satisfies Pooja's social and psychological needs such as sense of belongingness, giving and receiving attention, love and power through this group.

(iv) **Goal Achievement** This group helps in achieving the goals of Pooja which she can not achieve individually.

(v) **Provide Knowledge and Information** As individual Pooja may not have all the required information about the dance competitions. Group supplements her the necessary information and knowledge.

6. Describe the element of group structure.

Ans. There are four important elements of group structure which are as follows

(i) **Roles** Roles refer to the typical behaviour that depicts a person in a given social context. These are socially defined expectations that individuals in a given situation are expected to fulfil.

(ii) **Norms** These are expected standards of behaviour and beliefs established, agreed upon, and enforced by group members. They may be considered as a group's 'unspoken rules'.

(iii) **Status** It refers to the relative social position given to group members by others. This relative position or status may be either ascribed (given may be because of one's seniority) or achieved (the person has achieved status because of expertise or hard work). By being members of the group, we enjoy the status associated with that group.

(iv) **Cohesiveness** It refers to togetherness, binding, or mutual attraction among group members. As the group becomes more cohesive, group members start to think, feel and act as a social unit and less like isolated individuals.

7. Distinguish between primary and secondary group.

Ans. A major difference between primary and secondary groups are as follows

Primary Groups	Secondary Groups
Primary group are pre-existing formations which are usually given to the individual.	Secondary group are those which the individual joins by choice.
Family, caste, and religion are examples of primary groups.	Membership of a political party is an example of a secondary group.
In a primary group, there is a face-to-face interaction, members have close physical proximity, and they share warm emotional bonds.	In secondary groups relationships among members are more impersonal, indiect, and less frequent.
Primary groups are central to individual's functioning and have a very major role in developing values and ideals of the individual during the early stages of development.	Secondary groups did not play an important role in developing values and ideals.
In the primary group, boundaries are less permeable, i.e. members do not have the option to choose its membership as compared to secondary groups.	In secondary groups it is easy to leave and join another group.

8. Compare and contrast formal and informal groups and ingroups and outgroups. **(NCERT)**

Ans. We can compare formal group with informal group and ingroup with outgroup in the following ways

Formal Groups

(i) The functions of a formal group are explicitly stated in the case of an office organisation.

(ii) The roles of its group members are well defined.

(iii) The formal groups is based on some specific rules or law. For example, a university.

Informal Groups

(i) Informal decision-making process may exist as parallel mechanism.

(ii) Members of this group have a close relationship and take decision in informal settings.

(iii) There are no strict rules and regulation for this group.

Ingroups

(i) It is generally considered as me, my, we or our group.

(ii) People in ingroup are viewed as having desirable behaviour and admirable traits.

(iii) It is always good, strong, cohesive.

Outgroup

(i) It is considered as 'they' group.

(ii) Members are often perceived negatively.

(iii) It is always people with damaging, dangerous and negative emotions.

9. Who discovered the process of Groupthink. Also discuss about the process of groupthink.

Ans. **Irving Janis** discovered a process known as **groupthink** in which a group allows its concerns for unanimity. They override the motivation to realistically appraise courses of action. It results in the tendency of decision makers to make irrational and uncritical decisions.

Groupthink suggests the appearance of consensus or unanimous agreement within a group. All members of a group agree upon a particular decision of the group. No one express dissenting (expressing) opinion as it can destroy the cohesion of the group.

There are also some ways to prevent groupthink. These are as follows

• Encouraging and rewarding critical thinking.

• Encouraging groups to present alternative courses of action.

• Inviting outside experts to evaluate the group's decisions.

• Encouraging members to seek feedback from trusted others.

10. Differentiate between ingroup and outgroup.

Ans. The main differences between ingroup and outgroup are as follows

Ingroup	Outgroup
The term ingroup refers to one's own group. For ingroup members, we use the word 'we'.	Outgroup refers to another group. For outgroup members, the word 'they' is used.
It has been found that persons in the ingroup are generally supposed to be similar, are viewed favourably, and have desirable traits.	Members of the outgroup are viewed differently and are often perceived negatively in comparison to the ingroup members.
Members of the ingroup are are often perceived positively.	Members of the outgroup are viewed differently and are often perceived negatively in comparison to the ingroup members.

11. What is meant by social loafing? Give suitable examples. **(All India 2015, Delhi 2017)**

Or Explain the phenomenon of 'social loafing' by giving examples.

Ans. Social loafing is a phenomenon in which an individual work less hard in a group than they do when performing alone.

Social loafing is a reduction in individual effort when working on a collective task, i.e. one in which outputs are combined with those of other group members. Such situations give opportunities to group members to relax and become a free rider.

An example of such a task is the game of tug-of-war. It is not possible for you to identify how much force each member of the team has been exerting. Such situations give opportunities to group members to relax and become a free rider.

• Long Answer (LA) Type Questions

1. What is group? Explain giving examples the stages of group formation.

Ans A group may be defined as an organised system of two or more interdependent individuals, who have common motives and norms to regulate the behaviour of its members.

Tuckman suggested five stages of group. These are as follows

(i) **Forming** When group members meet for first time, a kind of uncertainty is created for achieving group goals. People try to know each other and assess whether they will fit in or not. There is excitement as well as apprehensions. This stage is called the forming stage.

(ii) **Storming** After forming stage, there is a stage of intragroup conflict which is referred to as storming. In this stage, there is conflict among

members about target, process, performance and control, resources. When this stage is complete, some sort of hierarchy of leadership in the group develops.

(iii) **Norming** The storming stage is followed by another stage known as norming. Group members by this time develop norms related to group behaviour. This leads to development of a positive group identity.

(iv) **Performing** By this stage the structure of the group has evolved and is accepted by group members. The group moves towards achieving the group goal. For some groups, this may be the last stage of group development.

(v) **Adjourning** In this stage, once the function is over, the group may be disbanded. However, all groups do not always proceed from one stage to the next in same manner.

2. What are the major types of Groups? Discuss in detail. **(NCERT)**

Ans. Major types of groups are discussed below

Primary and Secondary Groups Primary groups are pre-existing formations, which are usually given to the individual. In a primary group, there is a face to face interaction, members have close physical proximity and they share warm emotional bonds.

Secondary groups are those which the individual joins by choice. Membership of a political party is an example of a secondary group. Secondary groups are those where relationships among members are more impersonal, indirect and less frequent. In secondary groups, it is easy to leave and join another group.

Formal and Informal Groups The formation of formal groups is based on some specific rules or laws and members have definite roles. There are a set of norms which help in establishing order.

The formation of informal groups is not based on rules or laws and there is close relationship among members.

Ingroup and Outgroup The term ingroup refers to one's own group and outgroup refers to another group. For ingroup members, we use the word 'we' while for outgroup members, the word 'they' is used. By using the words we and they, one is categorising people as similar or different.

3. How can you reduce social loafing in groups? Think of any two incidents of social loafing in school. How did you overcome it? **(NCERT)**

Ans. Social loafing is a negative group influence which occurs due to defusion of responsibility.

It is a reduction in individual effort when working on a collective task, i.e. one in which outputs are pooled with those of other group members.

Two incidents of social loafing in school are as follows

(i) Some students work very less in group projects and works.

(ii) Sometimes during sports competition, some students practice very less and thus this affect the whole team.

Some measures to reduce social loafing are as follows

- Making the efforts of each person identifiable.
- Increasing the pressure to work hard (making group members committed to successful task performance).
- Increasing the apparent importance or value of a task.
- Making people feel that their individual contribution is important.
- Strengthening group cohesiveness which increases the motivation for successful group outcome.

4. Explain group polarisation. Give reasons for occurrence of group polarisation. **(CBSE 2018)**

Ans Group polarisation focuses on how groups usually make decisions that are more extreme than the original thoughts and views of the individual team members. It refers to the tendency for a group to make decisions that are more extreme than the initial inclination of its members.

For example, suppose you favour capital punishment for heinous crimes and you were interacting this issue with like-minded people. After this interaction, your views may become stronger as a result of group interaction and discussion.

Group polarisation occurs because of the following three reasons

(i) In the company of like-minded people, you are likely to hear newer arguments favouring your viewpoints.

(ii) When you find others also favouring capital punishment, you feel that this view is validated by the public. This is a sort of bandwagon effect.

(iii) When you find people having similar views, you are likely to perceive them as ingroup. You start identifying with the group, begin showing conformity and as a consequence your views become strengthened.

• Case Based Questions

1. A group may be defined as an organised system of two or more interdependent individuals, who have common motives and norms to regulate the behaviour of its members. A group not only provides us the needed support and comfort but also facilitates our growth and development as an individual.

Our lives are influenced by the nature of group membership we have. It is very important to be a part of a group which influences us positively and helps us in becoming good citizens. It is not only that others influence us, but we as individuals are also capable of changing others and the society. Similarly, we would try to understand group

conflicts and strategies to resolve conflicts for a harmonious and united society.

(i) What are the salient features seen in a group?

Ans. The salient features seen in a group are as follows

- It is a social unit consisting of two or more individuals who perceive themselves as belonging to the group.
- It is a collection of individuals who have common motives and goals.
- It is a collection of individuals who are interdependent, i.e. what one is doing may have consequences for others.
- Individuals who are trying to satisfy a need through their joint association also influence each other.

(ii) What do you mean by the terms crowd, teams and audience?

Ans. The terms crowd teams and audience are as follows

Crowd A crowd is a collection of people who may be present at a place/situation by chance. Behaviour of people in crowds is irrational and there is no interdependence among members

Teams These are special kinds of groups. Members of teams often have complementary skills and are committed to a common goal or purpose.

Audience It is a collection of people who have assembled for a special purpose, e.g. to watch a cricket match or a movie.

(iii) Explain the reasons why people join a group?

Ans. **Security** Groups reduce the feeling of insecurity when we are alone.

Status When we are members of a group that is perceived to be important by others, we feel recognised and experience a sense of power.

Self-esteem Groups provide feelings of self-worth and establish a positive social identity. Being a member of prestigious groups enhances one's self-concept.

Goal Achievement Groups help in achieving such goals which cannot be attained individually. There is power in the majority.

2. Social loafing occurs due to failure on the part of the individual worker, not any failure on the part of the collective. It has to do with members of the group feeling less pressure to perform because there are others to share the burden. This viewpoint is likely to breed resentment within the group and reduce overall performance even more. Some example of social loafing are discuss below

- Restaurant employees failing to put in equal amounts of effort is an example of social loafing. If there is a small number of customers present then all the servers need not work even if they are all on duty, so lazier workers will let the 'in' group take on all the responsibility.

- Have you ever been at a concert or an event where the main speaker asks the audience to say something or maybe clap? This is a perfect place for social loafing to happen. Sometimes the speaker may even say "That wasn't loud enough". Interestingly, the same thing happens as tug of war; as you add more people to a group, they are less likely to participate in what the speaker is asking them to do.

- Another example of social loafing in the workplace is simply logging off when members of your team step up to complete the daily tasks shared in a meeting. When you're in a Zoom conference room of 100, it's easier to feel like you can turn your camera off, grab a snack, or zone out.

(i) What are the reasons for the occurrence of social loafing?

Ans. Some reasons for the occurrence of social loafing are as follows

- Group members feel less responsible for the overall task being performed and therefore exert less effort.
- Motivation of members decreases because they realise that their contributions will not be evaluated on an individual basis.
- The performance of the group is not to be compared with other groups.

(ii) Give some measures to reduce social loafing?

Ans. Some measures to reduce social loafing are

- Making the efforts of each person identifiable.
- Increasing the pressure to work hard (making group members committed to successful task performance).
- Increasing the apparent importance or value of a task.
- Making people feel that their individual contribution is important.
- Strengthening group cohesiveness which increases the motivation for successful group outcome.

(iii) What was the experiment of Latane? Explain.

Ans. How much noise people make in social settings this phenomenon has been demonstrated in many experiments by Latane and his associates. They asked a group of male students to clap or cheer as loudly as possible because they wanted. The result revealed that although the total amount of noise rose up, the amount of noise produced by each participant dropped.

3. Rajesh, Kumar and Sameer, formed a group years ago when they wanted to open a small restaurant. The three of them invested an equal amount of money and shared the profit earned from it equally. Soon their business grew and they eventually opened a chain of restaurants. They still divide the profits equally and are best of friends. They manage the staff, the daily problems and the customers together. If at all an argument breaks in they dissolve it and let nothing come over their business.

(ii) Describe the factors which helped Rajesh, Kumar and Sameer to interact during the formation of their group.

Ans. Various factors that help Rajesh, Kumar and Sameer to interact during the formation of their group are proximity similarity and common motives and goals. These are discussed as follows

- **Proximity** Repeated interactions with the same set of individuals give us a chance to know them and their interests and attitudes.
- **Similarity** Being exposed to someone over a period of time makes us assess our similarities and paves the way for formation of groups.
- **Common** Motives and Goals: When people have common motives or goals, they get together and form a group which may facilitate their goal attainment.

(ii) Describe in detail various stages of group formation.

Ans. Tuckman suggested that groups pass through five developmental sequences. These are as follows

(i) **Forming** When group members meet for the first time, a kind of uncertainty is created for achieving group goals.

(ii) **Storming** After forming a stage, there is a stage of intragroup conflict which is referred to as storming.

(iii) **Norming** The storming stage is followed by another stage known as norming.

(iv) **Performing** By this stage the structure of the group has evolved and is accepted by group members.

(v) **Adjourning** In this stage, once the function is over, the group may be disbanded.

(iii) Explain four important elements of group structure.

Ans. The four important elements of the group structure are as follows

1. **Roles** These are socially defined expectations that individuals in a given situation are expected to fulfil.

2. **Norms** These are expected standards of behaviour and beliefs established, agreed upon and enforced by group members.

3. **Status** It refers to the relative social position given to group members by others.

4. **Cohesiveness** It refers to togetherness, binding or mutual attraction among group members.

Chapter Test

Multiple Choice Questions

1. Which of the following is an example of a group?
   - (a) Family
   - (b) Class
   - (c) Playground
   - (d) All of these

2. People join group for the reason of
   - (a) Security
   - (b) Status
   - (c) Self-esteem
   - (d) All of these

3. Group usually go through stages of
   - (a) Formation
   - (b) Conflict
   - (c) Performance
   - (d) All of these

4. Which of the following are not the element of group structures?
   - (a) Role
   - (b) Norms
   - (c) Status
   - (d) Expectations

5. A collection of people around a road side performer is an example of
   - (a) Crowd
   - (b) Group
   - (c) Mob
   - (d) Audience

Short Answer Type Questions

5. Explain in detail the concept of group think.
6. Who was Tuckman?
7. State some examples of primary groups.
8. Elaborate the term social loafing with examples.
9. Define the term social facilitation.
10. What do you understand by the term norm?

Long Answer Type Questions

11. Define Group. Mention its characteristics.
12. Describe conditions for the formation of group.
13. Are you a member of certain group? Discuss what motivated you to join that group.

Answers

1. (a)   *2.* (d)   *3.* (d)   *4.* (d)

Practice Papers
1-3

Practice Paper 1[*]
(Solved)

General Instructions

■ Time : **2 Hours**
■ Max. Marks : **35**

1. There are 9 questions in the question paper. All questions are compulsory.
2. Question no. 1 is a Case Based Question, which has five MCQs. Each question carries one mark.
3. Question no. 2-6 are Short Type Questions. Each question carries 3 marks.
4. Question no. 7-9 are Long Answer Type Questions. Each question carries 5 marks.
5. There is no overall choice. However, internal choice have been provided in some questions. Students have to attempt only on of the alternatives in such questions

---

** As exact Blue-print and Pattern for CBSE Term II exams is not released yet. So the pattern of this paper is designed by the author on the basis of trend of past CBSE Papers. Students are advised not to consider the pattern of this paper as official. It is just for practice purpose.*

Case Based Questions (5 Marks)

1. Read the given passage and answer the following questions.

Sangeeta is a 12-years-old schizophrenic girl. She behaves strangely and is not adequate at personal or social tasks. She often hears voices which do not exist. Sangeeta's speech is not very well developed. She speaks in a slow and sluggish manner. She also keeps on repeating the same things again and again. She often starts speaking something else in the middle of a conversation. She also invents new words which make no sense. Sangeeta also shows very less emotions like anger or sadness. There are times when she would remain in one single position for hours. Currently, she is consulting a psychiatrist but her condition has only been deteriorating. $(1 \times 5 = 5)$

(i) What type of hallucination is Sangeeta experiencing?
  (a) Auditory   (b) Visual   (c) Tactile   (d) Somatic

(ii) What is the lack of speech development in schizophrenics called?
  (a) Inattention   (b) Alogia   (c) Delusion   (d) Catatonia

(iii) Sangeeta shows very few emotions. What is this phenomenon called?
  (a) Flat affect   (b) Lack affect   (c) Blunted affect   (d) Sharp affect

(iv) Sangeeta keeps on repeating the same thoughts again and again. This situation of Sangeeta is called
  (a) Derailment   (b) Delusion   (c) Neologisms   (d) Perseveration

(v) **Assertion** (A) Sangeeta is known to sit motionless for hours.
  Reason (R) Such behaviour is commonly seen in schizophrenic patients.
  (a) Both A and R are true and R is the correct explanation of A
  (b) Both A and R are true, but R is not the correct explanation of A
  (c) A is true, but R is false
  (d) A is false, but R is true

Short Answer Questions (3 Marks)

2. What are the factors underlying abnormal behaviour? Explain any two factors in detail.

Or Name all the anxiety disorders and explain at least two anxiety disorders in detail.

3. What are the characteristics of psychotherapeutic approach?

Or What are the various parameters of classification of psychotherapy?

4. Explain valence and extremeness as the features of attitude.

Or Explain prejudice and discrimination with examples.

5. Explain the phenomenon of groupthink. Also write some ways to prevent groupthink.

6. Write a short note on social loafing. Why social loafing occur. Give reasons.

Long Answer Questions (5 Marks)

7. Explain the ancient theory of abnormal behaviour. Which approaches of abnormality are believed in the past? Discuss in detail.

Or Lalit is a software engineer and works in a reputed company. He has a notorious habit of eating too much. Recently, he gained 10 kgs while working on an important office project. Explain in detail various kinds of substance abuse.

8. Siyaan is a five-years-old boy whose parents used to give him a toffee everytime, he used to do something good. Gradually, they reduced the frequency of toffee. Now, they give him toffee sometimes for good behaviour but sometimes they just appreciate him. However, Siyaan's habit of behaving good has stayed irrespective of being given a toffee or not. Explain in detail various types of behavioural therapies.

Or Vaibhavi always thought less of herself as she was not earning as much as her sisters. The thought disturbed her so much that she gradually drifted towards depression. Explain in detail various types of cognitive therapies that could help Vaibhavi.

9. Explain the major concepts involved in the process of attitude change.

Or Social psychologists have shown various sources that lead to prejudices in society. Discuss these sources of prejudices in detail.

Answers

1. (i) (*a*) Sangeeta is experiencing auditory type of hallucination. This symptom is particularly associated with schizophrenia and related psychotic disorders.

(ii) (*b*) The lack of speech development in schizophrenics is called Alogia.

(iii) (*c*) The phenomenon of showing very few emotions by Sangeeta is called Blunted affect. Blunted affect is also referred to as emotional blunting. It is a prominent symptom of schizophrenia. Patients with blunted affect have difficulty in expressing their emotions.

(iv) (*d*) This situation of Sangeeta is called Perseveration.

(v) (*a*) People like Sangeeta who suffered from schizophrenia show psychomotor symptoms. They moveless spontaneously or make odd grimaces and gestures. These symptoms may take extreme forms known as catatonia. People in a catatonic stupor remain motionless and silent for long stretches of time. Hence, both A and R are true and R is the correct explanation of A.

2. Factors that underlying abnormal behaviour include

- Biological factors
- Genetic factors
- Psychological models
- Psychodynamic models
- Behavioural models
- Cognitive model
- Humanistic-existential model
- Socio-cultural model
- Diathesis-stress model

Two factors of abnormal behaviour are discussed as follows

Cognitive Model This model states that abnormal functioning can result from cognitive problems. People may hold assumptions and attitudes about themselves that are irrational and inaccurate. They may also repeatedly think in illogical ways. Sometimes they make over-generalisations and draw broad, negative conclusions on the basis of a single insignificant event.

Humanistic-Existential Model This model focuses on broader aspects of human existence. Humanists believe that human beings are born with a natural tendency to be friendly, cooperative and constructive. They are driven to self-actualise i.e. to fulfil this potential for goodness and growth. Existentialists believe that from birth we have total freedom to give meaning to our existence or to avoid that responsibility. Those who avoid the responsibility would live empty, inauthentic and dysfunctional lives.

Or

Following are the various types of anxiety disorders

- Generalised anxiety disorder
- Panic disorder
- Phobia
- Post-traumatic stress disorder
- Obsessive-compulsive disorder
- Separation anxiety disorder

Two anxiety disorders are discussed as follows

Generalised Anxiety Disorder It consists of continued, vague (unclear), unexplained and intense fears that are not attached to any particular object. The symptoms include worry and apprehensive feelings about the future, hypervigilance which involves constantly scanning the environment for dangers. It is marked by motor tension, as a result of which the person is unable to relax, is restless and visibly shaky (weak) and tense.

Panic Disorder It consists of recurrent anxiety attacks in which the person experiences intense terror. A panic attack denotes an abrupt rise of intense anxiety rising to a peak when thoughts of a particular stimuli are present.

Such thoughts occur in an unpredictable manner. The clinical features include shortness of breath, dizziness, trembling, palpitations, choking, nausea, chest pain or discomfort, fear of going crazy, losing control or dying.

3. Psychotherapeutic approaches have the following characteristics

- There is systematic application of principles underlying the different theories of therapy.
- Persons who have received practical training under expert supervision only can practice psychotherapy. An untrained person may unintentionally cause more harm than any good.
- The therapeutic situation involves a therapist and a client who seeks and receives help for her/his emotional problems.
- The interaction of these two persons i.e. the therapist and the client, results in the formation of the therapeutic relationship. This is a confidential, interpersonal and dynamic relationship. This human relationship is central to any sort of psychological therapy and is the vehicle for change.

Or

The classification of psychotherapies is based on the following parameters

1. Psychodynamic therapy views intrapsychic conflicts i.e. the conflicts that are present within the psyche of the person, are the sources of psychological problems.

2. In the psychodynamic therapy, unfulfilled desires of childhood and unresolved childhood fears lead to intrapsychic conflicts. The behaviour therapy suggested that faulty conditioning patterns, faulty learning and faulty thinking and beliefs lead to abnormal (maladaptive) behaviours that, in turn, lead to psychological problems.

3. Psychodynamic therapy uses the methods of free association and reporting of dreams to generate the thoughts and feelings of the client. This material is interpreted by the client to help her/him to confront and resolve the conflicts and thus overcome problems.

4. Nature of the Therapeutic Relationship between the Client and the Therapist Psychodynamic therapy assumes that the therapist understands the client's intrapsychic conflicts better than the client himself. The therapist interprets the thoughts and feelings of the client to her/him so that she/he gains an understanding of the same.

5. Chief Benefit to the Client Psychodynamic therapy values emotional insight as the important benefit that the client derives from the treatment.

4. **Valence** (Positivity or Negativity) as a **feature of attitude**

The valence of an attitude tells us whether an attitude is positive or negative towards the attitude object. A neutral attitude would have neither positive nor negative valence. For example, an attitude towards nuclear research has to be expressed on a 5 point scale, ranging from 1 (very bad), 2 (bad), 3 (neutral-neither good nor bad), 4 (good) and 5 (very good). If an individual rates his view as 1, 2 then it is negative attitude, if he rates 4 to 5 then it is positive attitude and if he rates 3 then it is neutral attitude i.e. neither positive nor negative valence.

Extremeness as a feature of attitude

The extremeness of an attitude indicates how positive or negative an attitude is. For example, if an individual rates the nuclear research as 1 or 5, these are regarded as extreme ratings. They are only in the opposite directions (valence). A neutral attitude is lowest on extremeness.

Or

Prejudices are examples of attitudes towards a particular group. They are usually negative and in many cases, may be based on stereotypes (the cognitive component) about the specific group. A stereotype is a cluster of ideas regarding the characteristics of a specific group. Stereotypes consist of undesirable characteristics about the target group and they lead to negative attitudes or prejudices towards members of specific groups.

Prejudice may also grew as discrimination. But prejudices can exist without showing discrimination. Similarly, discrimination can be shown without prejudice. Wherever prejudice and discrimination exist, conflicts are very likely to arise between groups within the same society.

For example, the genocide committed by the Nazis in Germany against Jewish people is an example of how prejudice can lead to hatred, discrimination and mass killing of innocent people. We get numerous examples from history containing discrimination based on race and caste on social class.

5. Irving Janis discovered a process known as 'group think'.In this process, a group allows its concerns for unanimity. They override the motivation to realistically appraise courses of action. It results in the tendency of decision makers to make irrational and uncritical decisions.

Groupthink suggests the appearance of consensus or unanimous agreement within a group. All members of a group agree upon a particular decision of the group. No one express dissenting opinion as it can destroy the cohesion of the group.

There are also some ways to prevent 'groupthink'. These are as follows

- Encouraging and rewarding critical thinking.
- Encouraging groups to present alternative courses of action.
- Inviting outside experts to evaluate the group's decisions.
- Encouraging members to seek feedback from trusted others.

6. Social loafing is a reduction in individual effort when working on a collective task, i.e. one in which outputs are combined with those of other group members. Such situations give opportunities to group members to relax and become a free rider.

This phenomenon has been demonstrated in many experiments by Latane and his associates.

Some reasons for the occurring of social loafing are as follows

- Group members feel less responsible for the overall task being performed and therefore exerting less effort.
- Motivation of members decreases because they realise that their contributions will not be evaluated on individual basis.
- The performance of the group is not to be compared with other groups.
- There is an improper coordination (or no coordination) among members.

- Belonging to the same group is not important for members. It is only an aggregate of individuals.

7. Ancient theory about abnormality holds that abnormal behaviour can be explained by the operation of supernatural and magical forces such as evil spirits (bhoot-pret) or the devil (shaitan). Exorcism i.e. removing the evil that resides in the individual through countermagic and prayer is still commonly used.

Various approaches of abnormality believed in the past included: Biological or Organic Approach. The history of abnormal psychology believed that individuals behave strangely because their bodies and their brains are not working properly. This is the biological or organic approach. In the modern era, there is evidence that body and brain processes have been linked to many types of maladaptive behaviour.

Following are the approaches of abnormality which are believed in the past.

Psychological Approach According to this point of view, psychological problems are caused by inadequacies in the way an individual thinks, feels or perceives the world.

Organismic Approach In the ancient Western world, philosophers and temperament physicians of ancient Greece such as Hippocrates, Socrates and Plato developed the organismic approach and viewed disturbed behaviour as arising out of conflicts between emotion and reason. Galen elaborated the role of the four humours in personal character and temperament.

Demonology and Superstition Demonology is related to a belief that people with mental problems were evil and there are numerous instances of 'describe witch hunts' during the middle age. In this period, demonology and superstition gained renewed importance in the explanation of abnormal behaviour.

The Renaissance Period was marked by increased humanism and curiosity about behaviour. Johann Weyer emphasised psychological conflict and disturbed interpersonal relationships as causes of psychological disorders.

Reforms of asylums were initiated in both Europe and America. The aspect of the reform movement was the new inclination for deinstitutionalisation which placed emphasis on providing community care for recovered mentally ill individuals.

Biopsychosocial Approach

In this approach, all three factors i.e. biological, psychological and social play important roles in influencing the expression and outcome of psychological disorders.

Or

Various types of substance disorders are as follows

1. **Alcohol Abuse and Dependence**

   People who abuse alcohol, drink large amounts of alcohol regularly and rely on it to help them face difficult situations. Drinking interferes with social behaviour and ability to think and work. For many people, the pattern of alcohol abuse extends to dependence i.e. their bodies build up a tolerance for alcohol and they need to drink even in greater amounts to feel its effects.

   Some effects of alcohol abuse are as follows

   - Alcoholism destroys millions of families, social relationships and careers. Intoxicated drivers are responsible for many road accidents.
   - It also has serious effects on the children of persons with this disorder.
   - These children have higher rates of psychological problems, particularly anxiety, depression, phobias and substance-related disorders.
   - Excessive drinking can seriously damage physical health.

2. **Heroin Abuse and Dependence**

   - Heroin intake significantly interferes with social and occupational functioning. Most abusers further develop a dependence on heroin and experience a withdrawal reaction when they stop taking it.
   - The most direct danger of heroin abuse is an overdose, which slows down the respiratory centres in the brain, almost paralysing breathing and in many cases causing death.

3. **Cocaine Abuse and Dependence**

   Regular use of cocaine may lead to a pattern of abuse in which the person may be intoxicated throughout the day and function poorly in social relationships and at work. It may also cause problems with short-term memory and attention. In case of dependency, cocaine dominates the person's life as more drugs are needed to get the desired effects and stopping it results in feelings of depression, fatigue, sleep problems, irritability and anxiety. Cocaine poses serious dangers. It has dangerous effects on psychological functioning and physical well-being.

8. There are various techniques for changing behaviour. Some techniques of behaviour modification are as follows

   Negative Reinforcement It is a major technique of behaviour modification. Responses that lead organisms to get rid of painful stimuli or avoid and escape from them provide negative reinforcement.

   Aversive Conditioning It refers to repeated association of undesired response with an adverse consequence. For example, an alcoholic is given a mild electric shock and asked to smell the alcohol.

Positive Reinforcement If an adaptive behaviour occurs rarely, positive reinforcement is given to increase the deficit. For example, if a child does not do homework regularly, positive reinforcement may be used by the child's mother by preparing the child's favourite dish whenever she/he does homework at the appointed time.

Token Economy Person with behavioural problems can be given a token as a reward every time when a wanted behaviour occurs. The tokens are collected and exchanged for a reward such as an outing for the patient or a treat for the child. This is known as token economy.

Differential Reinforcement Unwanted behaviour can be reduced and wanted behaviour can be increased simultaneously through differential reinforcement.

Systematic Desensitisation It is a technique introduced by Wolpe for treating phobias or irrational fears. The client is interviewed to generate fear-provoking situations.

Principle of Reciprocal Inhibition This principle states that the presence of two mutually opposing forces at the same time, inhibits the weaker force. Thus, the relaxation response is first built up and a mildly anxiety-provoking scene is imagined, through which the anxiety is overcome by the relaxation.

Modelling It is the procedure wherein the client learns to behave in a certain way by observing the behaviour of a role model or the therapist who initially acts as the role model. Vicarious learning i.e. learning by observing others, is used and through a process of rewarding small changes in the behaviour, the client gradually learns to acquire the behaviour of the model.

Or

Rational Emotive Therapy (RET), Aaron Beck's Cognitive Therapy and Cognitive Behaviour Therapy (CBT) can help Vaibhavi. These therapies revealed the cause of psychological distress in irrational thoughts and beliefs. These therapies are discussed as follows

Rational Emotive Therapy (RET)

It was formulated by Albert Ellis. The central idea of this therapy is that irrational beliefs mediate between the antecedent events and their consequences. The first step in RET is the Antecedent Belief-Consequence (ABC) analysis. Antecedent events, which caused the psychological distress are noted.

Aaron Beck's Cognitive Therapy

Aaron Beck gave another cognitive therapy. His theory of psychological distress is characterised by anxiety or depression. It states that childhood experiences provided by the family and society develop core schemas or systems, which include beliefs and action patterns in the individual. Negative thoughts which develop are persistent irrational thoughts. These are characterised by cognitive distortions. For example, 'Nobody loves me', 'I am ugly', 'I am stupid', etc.

Cognitive Behaviour Therapy (CBT)

CBT is the most popular therapy. It is a short and efficacious treatment for a wide range of psychological disorders such as anxiety, depression, panic attacks and borderline personality, etc. It adopts a biopsychosocial approach to the delineation (explain in detail) of psychopathology.

9. Three major concepts involved in the process of attitude change are described as follows

1. The Concept of Balance

It was proposed by Fritz Heider. It is also described in the form of the P-O-X triangle, which represents the relationships between three aspects or components of the attitude.

- P is the person whose attitude is being studied.
- O is another person.
- X is the topic towards which the attitude is being studied (attitude object).

Consider the example of dowry as an attitude topic (X). A person has a positive attitude toward dowry (P-X positive). P is planning to get his son married to the daughter of some person O. O has a negative attitude towards dowry (O-X negative). If O initially has a positive attitude towards P, the situation would be unbalanced. P-X is positive, O-P is positive but O-X is negative. This is a situation of imbalance.

2. The Concept of Cognitive Dissonance

It was proposed by Leon Festinger. It emphasises that the cognitive components of an attitude must be consonant (opposite of dissonant) i.e. they should be logically in line with each other. Festinger and Carlsmith, two social psychologists, conducted an experiment that showed the working of cognitive dissonance. Both balance and cognitive dissonance are examples of cognitive consistency.

3. The Two-Step Concept

It was proposed by SM Mohsin, an Indian psychologist. According to him, attitude change takes place in the form of two steps. These are as follows

(i) In the first step, the target of change identifies with the source. The target is the person whose attitude is to be changed. The source is the person through whose influence the change is to take place. Identification means that the target has liking and regard for the source. The source must also have a positive attitude towards the target and the regard and attraction becomes mutual.

(ii) In the second step, the source herself/himself shows an attitude change, by actually changing her/his behaviour towards the attitude object. Observing the source's changed attitude and behaviour, the target also shows an attitude change through behaviour. This is a kind of imitation or observational learning. One of the three attitudes will have to change to make the situation a situation of balance.

Or

Social psychologists have shown that prejudice has the following sources

- **Learning** Like other attitudes, prejudices can also be learned through association, reward and punishment, observing others, group or cultural norms and exposure to information that encourages prejudice. The family, reference groups, personal experiences and the media may play a role in the learning of prejudices. People who learn prejudiced attitudes may develop a 'prejudiced personality' and show low adjusting capacity, anxiety and feelings of hostility against the outgroup.

- **A Strong Social Identity and Ingroup Bias** Individuals who have a strong sense of social identity and have a very positive attitude towards their own group boost this attitude by holding negative attitudes towards other groups. These are shown as prejudices.

- **Scapegoating** This is a phenomenon by which the majority group places the blame on a minority outgroup for its own social, economic or political problems. The minority is too weak or too small in number to defend itself against such accusations (complaints). Scapegoating is a group based way of expressing frustration and it often results in negative attitudes or prejudice against the weaker group.

- **Kernel of Truth Concept** Sometimes people may continue to hold stereotypes because they think that there must be some truth or 'Kernel of Truth' in what everyone says about the other group.

- **Self-fulfilling Prophecy** In some cases, the group that is the target of prejudice is itself responsible for continuing the prejudice. The target group may behave in ways that justify the prejudice i.e. confirm the negative expectations.

Practice Paper 2[*]
(Unsolved)

General Instructions

- Time : **2 Hours**
- Max. Marks : **35**

1. There are 9 questions in the question paper. All questions are compulsory.
2. Question no. 1 is a Case Based Question, which has five MCQs. Each question carries one mark.
3. Question no. 2-6 are Short Type Questions. Each question carries 3 marks.
4. Question no. 7-9 are Long Answer Type Questions. Each question carries 5 marks.
5. There is no overall choice. However, internal choice have been provided in some questions.
   Students have to attempt only on of the alternatives in such questions

** As exact Blue-print and Pattern for CBSE Term II exams is not released yet. So the pattern of this paper is designed by the author on the basis of trend of past CBSE Papers. Students are advised not to consider the pattern of this paper as official. It is just for practice purpose.*

Case Based Questions (5 Marks)

1. Read the given passage and answer the following questions.

   Mr. John is a twenty-seven years old man who consulted a psychologist to discuss what he calls his 'silly habits'. He reports that for several years he had to check and recheck electrical appliances, as well as doors and windows, before leaving home each morning and again before going to bed. At times, the checking has made him late for work and has disturbed his sleep such that he had to get up to check everything several times yet again. When questioned about the reasons for this behaviour, Mr. John reported that he could not stop thinking that electrical appliances may short circuit and cause a disastrous fire or that his house may be broken into and he will lose all valuables. He recognises these concerns and the resulting checking as excessive and unreasonable yet feels compelled to do something to alleviate the anxiety associated with the thoughts. During counselling, the psychologist found out that some time before the checking rituals started, a major fire had broken in Mr. John's office and all important papers were destroyed. $(1 \times 5 = 5)$

   (i) Identify Mr. John's disorder.
   - (a) Generalised anxiety disorder
   - (b) Major depressive disorders
   - (c) Obsessive-compulsive disorder
   - (d) Somatic symptom disorder

   (ii) Which of the following statements represents his repetitive thoughts?
   - (a) For a number of years, he had to check and recheck electrical appliances.
   - (b) He had to get up to check everything a number of times.
   - (c) The checking has made him late for work.
   - (d) He could not stop thinking that electrical appliances may short circuit and cause a disastrous fire.

   (iii) Which disorder also comes under the category of obsessive-compulsive and related disorders?
   - (a) Excoriation disorder
   - (b) Acute stress disorder
   - (c) Adjustment disorder
   - (d) Cyclothymic disorder

(iv) Obsessive behaviour is the inability to stop thinking about a particular __________ .
    (a) idea or topic   (b) rule
    (c) person   (d) None of these

(v) People affected by obsessive-compulsive disorder are unable to prevent themselves from______.
    (a) repeatedly carrying out a particular act
    (b) sleeping in day
    (c) overeating
    (d) None of the above

Short Answer Questions (3 Marks)

2. Fatima is experiencing generalised anxiety disorder. Enumerate any two causes with reference to diathesis stress model which may have led to the disorder.

Or Differentiate between hostile aggression and proactive aggression.

3. How is behaviour therapy used to treat phobia?

Or Explain the ethical standards that need to be practised by psychotherapists.

4. What are simplicity and complexity features of attitude?

Or Rohit is a 7 years old boy. Which factors play a significant role in shaping his attitude formation?

5. Explain the reasons that make people join groups.

6. What is Bandwagon effect. Write in brief.

Long Answer Questions (5 Marks)

7. Veena has been getting rage attacks for the past one year. She has also been depressed for some time. Discuss in detail Veena's condition of bipolar mood disorder.

Or Sohail has been telling his parents that he has been seeing few things and hearing few voices which do not exist. Hence, Sohail is having hallucinations. Explain delusion and hallucination in detail.

8. Yoga and meditation both are important for health. Meditation is a part of yoga, which deals with mental relaxation and concentration. Write in detail about yoga and meditation.

Or Veni has just gone through an extensive treatment for her depression. She is currently in a rehabilitation center and she is being taught various skills to help her get out of the depressive situation. Explain in detail how Veni and other mentally ill patients can be given help by rehabilitation.

9. There are various factors that influence learning of an attitude. Explain these factors in detail.

Or Meenakshi has been facing prejudice at work because she is a female employee. Explain in detail various strategies for handling prejudices.

Answers

1.	*(i) (c)*	*(ii) (d)*	*(iii) (a)*	*(iv) (a)*	*(v) (a)*

Practice Paper 3[*]

(Unsolved)

General Instructions

- Time : **2 Hours**
- Max. Marks : **35**

1. There are 9 questions in the question paper. All questions are compulsory.
2. Question no. 1 is a Case Based Question, which has five MCQs. Each question carries one mark.
3. Question no. 2-6 are Short Type Questions. Each question carries 3 marks.
4. Question no. 7-9 are Long Answer Type Questions. Each question carries 5 marks.
5. There is no overall choice. However, internal choice have been provided in some questions. Students have to attempt only on of the alternatives in such questions

---

** As exact Blue-print and Pattern for CBSE Term II exams is not released yet. So the pattern of this paper is designed by the author on the basis of trend of past CBSE Papers. Students are advised not to consider the pattern of this paper as official. It is just for practice purpose.*

Case Based Questions (5 Marks)

1. Read the given passage and answer the following questions.

Raman washes his hands every time he touches something. One of his colleagues also observed that he washes even things like coins. He further noticed that Raman steps only within the patterns on the floor or road while walking. He also has the habit of stacking books and files on every table and gets annoyed with a little bit of mess. He even gets a duster to the office and repeatedly likes to wipe his desk. He does not like anyone eating around his desk. The habit is so intense that he loses a good amount of his working hours over his habit of cleaning and organising things. When the office counsellor spoke to Raman about it he denied any of such extensive behaviour and also refused to take any treatment for it. $(1 \times 5 = 5)$

(i) What is Raman suffering from?
   (a) Bipolar disorder
   (b) Dissociative amnesia
   (c) A general love for hygiene
   (d) Obsessive-compulsive disorder

(ii) Trichotillomania is a term used for
   (a) Skin-picking disorder
   (b) Hair-pulling disorder
   (c) Nail biting
   (d) Hoarding disorder

(iii) Which of the following symptoms is shown by Raman?
   (a) Mania
   (b) Depression
   (c) Tremors
   (d) Compulsive performance of an action

(iv) Why do you think Raman refused any treatment?
   (a) He does not want the stigma of psychological disorder.
   (b) He does not want to get cured.
   (c) He cannot afford the treatment.
   (d) He does not like medicines.

(v) **Assertion** (A) Compulsive behaviour is the need to perform certain behaviours over and over again.

Reason (R) Many compulsions deal with counting, ordering, checking, touching and washing.

Codes
(a) Both A and R are true and R is the correct explanation of A
(b) Both A and R are true, but R is not a correct explanation of A
(c) A is true, but R is false
(d) R is true, but A is false

Short Answer Questions (3 Marks)

2. Write a short note on obsessive-compulsive disorder.

Or Write a short note on trauma and stress related disorder.

3. Rajesh is an alcoholic patient with depression. How the alternative therapies can help him to overcome this difficulty?

Or Write a short note on relaxation procedures used in treating psychological disorders.

4. Write a short note on the relationship between attitude and behaviour.

Or Elaborate the ABC component of attitude.

5. Enumerate all the reasons for a person to join a group.

6. Explain the term role, status and cohesiveness in detail.

Long Answer Questions (5 Marks)

7. What are somatic symptoms and related disorders? Explain in detail.

Or Madhu suddenly is not able to remember anything from her past. This occurred after the sudden demise of her husband in an accident. Explain all the dissociative disorders in detail.

8. Medication can be provided by a certified psychiatrist to treat psychological disorders. Explain in detail about the biomedical therapy used for treating psychological disorders.

Or Discuss in detail the factors that contribute to healing in psychotherapy.

9. Saurabh is a young 9-years-old boy who is very mischievous but behaves very nicely in front of others. Throw some light on the change in behaviour that occurs in the presence of others.

Or Smriti likes to throw the leftover bread to the dogs who live in her lane. Explain pro-social behaviour in detail.

Answers

1.   (i) (d)   (ii) (b)   (iii) (d)   (iv) (a)   (v) (b)

Printed by Libri Plureos GmbH in Hamburg,
Germany